BOSWELL'S LITERARY ART

GARLAND REFERENCE LIBRARY
OF THE HUMANITIES
(VOL. 969)

BOSWELL'S LITERARY ART
An Annotated Bibliography of Critical Studies, 1900–1985

Hamilton E. Cochrane

GARLAND PUBLISHING, INC. • NEW YORK & LONDON
1992

Library of Congress Cataloging-in-Publication Data

Cochrane, Hamilton E., 1956–
Boswell's literary art : an annotated bibliography of critical studies, 1900–1985 / Hamilton E. Cochrane.
p. cm. — (Garland reference library of the humanities ; vol. 969)
Includes index.
ISBN 0–8240–1516–9
1. Boswell, James, 1740–1795—Criticism and interpretation—Bibliography. I. Title. II. Series.
Z8110.2.C63 1992
[PR3325] 91–30751
016.828'609—dc20 CIP

Printed on acid-free, 250-year-life paper
Manufactured in the United States of America

Contents

Preface

Boswell's Literary Art is an annotated bibliography of secondary sources in English--books, scholarly articles, dissertations--published between 1900 and 1985. The primary focus, reflected both in the selection of sources and in the annotations, is Boswell as a writer and his major literary achievements: the Life of Johnson, Tour to the Hebrides, and the journals.

Many sources that are not primarily critical in nature, however, have been included: biographies, for example, personality sketches, studies of Boswell's legal career. This has been done, first, because there is no clear-cut division between biography and criticism in Boswell scholarship. Boswell's attitude toward Johnson, traits such as honesty and diligence, the playing of roles--these enter both biographical and critical studies. Further, some of the most important discussions of Boswell's art are found in biographical studies, from Chauncey Tinker's Young Boswell to Frederick Pottle and Frank Brady's monumental two-volume biography. In annotating such works, I have focused on the critical insights they provide into Boswell's literary achievement. A final justification for this inclusiveness is the recognition that literary studies ranging widely across disciplines and investigations--into the relationship of literature and the law, for example--are increasingly common. Even early accounts of Boswell's legal writing, then, may serve as important beginning points for further studies and are thus included here.

For the most part, the bibliography does not include reviews; articles in newspapers, newsletters, and popular magazines; imitations or dramatizations. I have made it my policy, however, to err, if I do, on the side of inclusiveness, and there are, therefore, some exceptions. I have included reviews of exceptional interest, either because of their authors--say, W.H. Auden's New Yorker piece on the London Journal--or because they make important contributions to an understanding of Boswell's art and the critical issues surrounding it--Donald J. Greene's review of Marshall Waingrow's edition of The Correspondence and Other Papers Relating to the Making of the Life of Johnson and Brady's review of William R. Siebenschuh's Fictional Techniques and Factual Works are prime examples.

Critical introductions to new editions of Boswell's works and to anthology selections have likewise not been included, again with some exceptions, the most notable being The Yale Edition of the Private Papers of James Boswell. These critical introductions by the best Boswell scholars of the twentieth century--Pottle, Brady, W.K. Wimsatt, Irma Lustig--deserve to be annotated because they are important critical essays in their own right, the starting point for any further critical examination of the journals and correspondence. In the case of some of the later volumes, these introductions represent nearly the only critical discussion of these particular portions of the journal.

The bibliography is divided into six major sections: Biographical Studies, Bibliographical Studies, Accounts of The Boswell Papers, Studies of Particular Works (subdivided as Life of Johnson, Journal of a Tour to the Hebrides, An Account of Corsica, Journals, Correspondence, and Miscellaneous Writings), General Studies, and Studies of Boswell and Other Topics (Religion, Politics, and Law). The entries within each section are arranged chronologically, in part, to tell more clearly the story of twentieth-century readers' evolving responses to Boswell and deepening understanding of his art. Articles that have been reprinted, excerpted, or anthologized in collections are listed in the year of their original publication and cross-referenced. A reader should be aware that these divisions are not absolute. A student of the Life, for example, should consult not only that section but also the index to locate pertinent works in other sections as well--biographical studies that include some critical commentary, general studies that discuss the Life in the context of Boswell's complete works, a notice about the Boswell papers that describes the manuscript of the Life.

In compiling the bibliography I have consulted the following sources: MLA Bibliography, Dissertations Abstracts International, The Eighteenth Century: A Current Bibliography, New Cambridge Bibliography of English Literature, Anthony Brown's Boswellian Studies: A Bibliography (Archon, 1972), James L. Clifford and Donald J. Greene's Samuel Johnson: A Survey and Bibliography of Critical Studies (University of Minnesota Press, 1970), Donald J. Greene and John A. Vance's A Bibliography of Johnsonian Studies, 1970-1985 (University of Victoria, 1987), and Paul J. deGategno's "The Scottish Enlightenment: A Bibliography of Doctoral Dissertations, 1965-1986" (Eighteenth-Century Scotland, volumes 1 and 2). In addition, I have read backwards through the notes and bibliographies in the studies I have located, beginning with John A. Vance's Boswell's Life of Johnson: New Questions, New Answers, and have in this way identified those sources cited by Boswell scholars.

It is conventional for a volume such as this one to include a critical introduction that surveys the scholarship, describing trends, noting landmark studies, and calling attention to the questions that have to be explored. In the case of twentieth-century Boswell scholarship, however, such an essay is unnecessary; the task has already been ably performed by two eminent students of Boswell. James L. Clifford's introduction to Twentieth-Century Interpretations of Boswell's Life of Johnson (Item 217) examines the criticism until 1970, and John Vance's introduction to Boswell's Life of Johnson: New Questions, New Answers (Item 279) surveys studies published between 1970 and 1985. A reader desiring to be acquainted with Boswell scholarship would do well to begin with these two essays.

Acknowledgments

This project could not have been completed without the generous support of Dr. Walter G. Sharrow, Canisius College Dean of Arts and Sciences, and Dr. Keith Burich, Acting Dean of Arts and Sciences during Dr. Sharrow's sabbatical, who funded my work through two summer terms. I wish to acknowledge also the support of the Dana Foundation, and in particular Rev. Edmund J. Ryan, S.J., the Canisius College Project Director, for awarding me two research grants. I have been aided immeasurably by these two superb Dana Grant research assistants: Wendy Gorski, who typed hundreds of cards and photocopied scores of articles, filled out loan requests, searched bibliographies, set up a computer file, and drafted a number of annotations, all with quiet thoroughness and absolute accuracy; and Kim Marie Romani, who likewise spent long hours at the computer, filled out still more loan requests, and double-checked entries with great skill and seemingly endless reserves of good cheer.

I am especially grateful to a number of other people who assisted me along the way. William R. Siebenschuh, who originally defined the book's scope and purpose, recommended me to complete the project, and Phyllis Korper has been my editor at Garland. Sally DiCarlo, Canisius College Interlibrary Loan Technician, processed what must have seemed like an alarming number of blue and white slips and showed herself again and again willing to go to any lengths to locate a fugitive piece. The Canisius College reference librarians, especially Pat McGlynn and Karen Bordonaro, have offered me valuable guidance and performed a number of computer searches. Colby Kullman, William Epstein, and Paul J. deGategno answered my queries promptly and provided me with material I could not have otherwise acquired. Cathy Bacon, Jack Schweigel, Jim Vallone, and Jim Dolan have provided computer instruction, advice, and calm responses to sometimes panicked questions. And, finally, Mary Cochrane brought her characteristic professionalism to the task of editing the final manuscript.

Boswell's Literary Art

BIOGRAPHICAL STUDIES

1. Filon, Augustin. "Boswell's Love Story." Fortnightly Review 86, n.s. 80 (1906): 487-95.

   Describes Boswell's relationship with Zélide as a "most interesting" example of "the duel between man and woman commonly called love."

2. Brown, J.T.T. "The Youth and Early Manhood of James Boswell." Proceedings of the Royal Philosophical Society of Glasgow 41 (1909-1911): 219-45.

   Reviews Boswell's life from 1758 to 1768--from his first visit to London and early publications through his meeting Johnson and making the Grand Tour to the beginnings of his legal career and the writing of Corsica--characterizing the period as an "unbroken course of literary development and the preparation for the life task"--the writing of the Life.

3. Glover, T.R. "Boswell." Poets and Puritans. London: Methuen and Co., 1916. 175-210.

   Provides a biographical sketch of Boswell with particular attention to his meeting, friendship, and travels with Johnson.

4. M., F.D. "Boswell: Executions, a Query." Times Literary Supplement, 13 Apr. 1922: 44.

   Inquires as to the truth of the story that Boswell rented a window by the year in Edinburgh in order to view executions.

5. Tinker, Chauncey B. "Boswell Takes a Wife." Atlantic Monthly, Feb. 1922: 157-66. Reprint. Item 6.

   Recounts Boswell's courtship of Kate Blair, Zélide, Mary Anne Boyd, and Margaret Montgomerie.

6. Tinker, Chauncey B. Young Boswell. Boston: Atlantic Monthly, 1922. Excerpt reprinted in Item 216.

   Contains a collection of connected biographical essays (including Items 51, 89), based largely on hitherto unpublished material and focusing on topics such as Boswell's travels; his relationship with Rousseau, Voltaire, and Wilkes; his search for a wife; and the composition of the Life. Suggests that Boswell, despite his literary genius, had not been treated seriously or sympathetically by earlier biographers in part because he--and especially his sense of humor--was misunderstood: Boswell did not mind offering himself as the butt so long as people laughed; thus, "the story of James Boswell is for those who are ready and able to realise that greatness may be linked with folly or, indeed, spring out of it."

7. Pottle, Frederick A. " 'Bozzy' Was a Bold Young Blade: Story of His Lady Mackintosh Episode Based on Unpublished Material." New York Times Book Review, 23 Aug. 1925: 1, 13.

Chronicles Boswell's intimacy with Lady Anne Mackintosh.

8. Strachey, Lytton. "James Boswell." New Republic, 4 Feb. 1925: 283-85. Reprint. Portraits in Miniature. New York: Harcourt, Brace and Co., 1931. 86-95. Biographical Essays. New York: Harcourt, Brace and Co., 1949. 147-52.

Portrays Boswell as "an idler, a lecher, a drunkard, and a snob," without dignity, pride, or shame, yet blessed with the qualities of a great biographer: psychological penetration, literary facility, a "passion for personalities." Concludes that it was the same force--Boswell's insatiable appetite for life--that led him to personal ruin and literary immortality.

9. Scott, Geoffrey. The Portrait of Zélide. New York: Scribners, 1927, 1959. 30-47.

Devotes a chapter of this biography of Belle de Zuylen to Boswell's courtship of her. Suggests that she was attracted by his "disarming honest absurdity" but was not willing to be molded into the devoted, orthodox, and decorous wife he sought.

10. Tinker, Chauncey B., and Frederick A. Pottle. A New Portrait of James Boswell. Cambridge: Harvard University Press, 1927.

Attributes to George Willison a hitherto unreproduced portrait of Boswell at the age of twenty-four and reproduces it along with portraits of Boswell by Reynolds, George Dance, Sir Thomas Lawrence, George Langton, J. Miller, Henry Singleton, and John Opie.

11. Salpeter, Harry. Dr. Johnson and Mr. Boswell. New York: Coward-McCann, 1929.

Provides a popular, illustrated portrait of Boswell's life and friendship with Johnson.

12. Vulliamy, C.E. James Boswell. London: Geoffrey Bles, 1932; New York: Scribners, 1933.

    Recounts Boswell's life in light of four ruling passions: wine, women, the desire for literary fame, and the desire to be acquainted with the great and notorious. Considers Boswell neither the fool described by Macaulay nor the literary genius celebrated by twentieth-century critics: neither a great man, a great thinker, nor a great writer, he was instead a man with a retentive memory and a gift for reproducing dialogue. Suggests that Boswell's later years are evidence of "mental and moral abnormality" and that his early worship of Johnson gave way to "a calculated policy of exploitation," arguing that Boswell associated with Johnson only as a way to prove his own personal value.

13. Pottle, Frederick A. Boswell and the Girl From Botany Bay. New York: Viking Press, 1937.

    Tells the story of Mary Broad, who was convicted for robbery in 1786, transported to Botany Bay, Australia, and escaped in 1791 with her husband, two children, and seven other convicts to the Dutch island of Timor, where they were eventually arrested and returned to England. Boswell befriended her; appealed on her behalf to Henry Dundas, who pardoned her; and supplied her with funds.

14. Quennell, Peter. "Boswell's Progress." Horizon (Dec. 1942): 394-403; (June 1943): 422-30; (July 1943): 45-54.

    Provides a sketch of Boswell's life and character, focusing on his relations with Rousseau, Voltaire, Paoli, Johnson, and Lonsdale; characterizes his life as a search for self-knowledge, self-mastery, and "real life." Emphasizes the heroic effort required to complete the Life and praises Boswell's biographical method as the best way to convey the complexity of human personality.

15. Quennell, Peter. "James Boswell." Four Portraits: Studies of the Eighteenth Century. London: William Collins Sons, 1945. 11-75. The Profane Virtues: Four Studies of the Eighteenth Century. New York: Viking. 1945. 1-63. Reprint. Hamden, CT: Archon Books, 1965. 15-78.

    Provides a brief life of Boswell, considering 1763 a decisive point--as it was also for the other subjects of the book--and focusing on those traits he shared with Gibbon, Sterne, and Wilkes: "vitality," "versatility," "devotion both to the pleasures of the world and to the satisfactions of the intellect."

16. Lewis, D.B. Wyndham. The Hooded Hawk, or the Case of Mr. Boswell. London: Eyre and Spottiswoode, 1946.

Provides a biographical account of Boswell's life meant to answer those who see him only as a drunkard and rake. Notes that in a narcissistic age, he was egotistical and pompous, but also likable and affectionate. Finds in "the hooded hawk," the symbol on the Boswell family crest, an appropriate emblem of the man: "perpetually attempting to soar into the empyrean, clogged by his own tirings, and perpetually falling to earth again, baffled."

17. Vulliamy, C.E. Ursa Major: A Study of Dr. Johnson and His Friends. London: Michael Joseph, 1946. 64-86, 246-67, 296-314.

Argues that Boswell was of no special importance to Johnson and describes Boswell as "peculiar" and "odd": an exhibitionist, a psychopathic personality "forever in flight from himself." Reconciles the apparent contradiction between Boswell's folly and weakness and the greatness of the Life by claiming the only remarkable parts of the book are the conversations, which required only diligence--not literary genius--to record accurately.

18. Hitschmann, Edward. "Boswell: The Biographer's Character." Psychoanalytic Quarterly 17 (1948): 212-25. Reprint. Great Men: Psychoanalytic Studies. New York: International University Press, 1956. 186-98.

Reviews psychological speculations of Boswell's early biographers and offers a new diagnosis: Boswell was a "psychopathic personality," his abnormality characterized by unusual creativity but also "self-destructive tendencies, social maladoption, unpredictable behavior, intense narcissism, and a weak ego," the result of his suffering the contempt and "unfeeling harshness" of his domineering father. Boswell felt "paricidal impulses" accompanied by strong feelings of guilt. Unable to identify with his father, Boswell "showed feminine qualities," his promiscuity perhaps "a defense against unconscious homosexual trends." Among Boswell's "compensatory corrections" was his search for a father substitute among great men, most notably Johnson, who evoked in Boswell ambivalent feelings--both admiration and animosity--apparent in the Life.

19. Mossner, Ernest Campbell. "Dr. Johnson: In Partibus Infidelium?" Modern Language Notes 63 (1948): 516-19.

Believes that although Boswell was Hume's tenant in an apartment at James's Court in 1773, by the time of Johnson's visit to Edinburgh, he had sublet those rooms and moved to another apartment on the same stair.

20. Lynd, Robert. "Boswell." Essays on Life and Literature. New York: E.P. Dutton and Co., 1951. 71-86.

Describes Boswell as an egotist, though one as fascinated with other people as much as with himself, and as "a bundle of contradictions"--by turns cheerful and depressed, torn between a genuine devotion to religion and morality and an appetite for sensual indulgence. Notes that Boswell's friendship with Johnson was founded on shared religious principles and pious intentions, and speculates that Johnson, despite his occasional protests, enjoyed being interrogated by Boswell.

21. Hoover, Andrew G. "Boswell's First London Visit." Virginia Quarterly Review 29 (1953): 242-56.

Publishes for the first time a letter from Boswell to Dalrymple that recounts his flight from the University of Glasgow to London in 1760. Describes Boswell's short-lived conversion to Roman Catholicism, Lord Eglinton's introducing him to the pleasures of London society, and his new acquaintances--Garrick, Sterne, Davies, and the Dodsleys.

22. Ansdell, Ora Joye. "Boswell of Scotland: The Importance of the Years Among His Countrymen in Developing His Character." Dissertation, University of Colorado at Boulder, 1956.

Studies the influence on Boswell of Scotland's economic, intellectual, and religious changes, and of his father, whom Boswell tried unsuccessfully to emulate. Finds in Boswell's journals and letters a conflict between his nature--emotional, imaginative, changeable--and what he aspired to be--rational, disciplined, sensible.

23. Lucas, F.L. "Boswell." The Search for Good Sense: Four Eighteenth-Century Characters: Johnson, Chesterfield, Boswell, Goldsmith. New York: Macmillan, 1958. 177-282.

Sketches Boswell's life and literary reputation, maintaining that he was neither the fool portrayed by Macaulay nor the Shakespearian genius described by twentieth-century critics.

24. Pearson, Hesketh. Johnson and Boswell: The Story of Their Lives. London: Heinemann, 1958.

Provides biographical accounts of Johnson and Boswell, focusing on their time together and emphasizing Boswell's penchant for self-dramatization, his "lack of a salient characteristic," and his need for the certainty Johnson provided. Claims that Boswell's chief fault as a biographer was his lack of a "selective sense," his mistaken belief that everything about Johnson was interesting, causing him to swell the Life to twice the length it ought to be.

25. Brooks, A. Russell. "Pleasure and Spiritual Turmoil in Boswell." *College Language Association Journal* 3 (1959): 12-19.

Argues that Boswell's "philosophy of pleasure"--his belief that a successful life consisted of vivid physical, intellectual, and spiritual sensations--was at the root of his spiritual conflict: he was unable to reconcile his religious convictions with his own practice; troubled by his own inability to control his behavior and moods, he became obsessed with the question of necessity; and terrified by the prospect of oblivion, by the end of all pleasurable sensation, he dreaded death.

26. Howes, Victor. "Boswell and Pseudo-Events." Christian Science Monitor, 5 Feb. 1963: 8.

Suggests that the most memorable scenes in Boswell's life--when he thrusts himself upon eminent people and interrogates them--are what the American historian Daniel Boorstin calls "pseudo-events": carefully planned occurrences, most often interviews, done for the purpose of being reproduced and intended to be self-fulfilling prophecies.

27. Pottle, Frederick A. "Boswell's University Education." Johnson, Boswell and Their Circle: Essays Presented to Lawrence Fitzroy Powell in Honour of His Eighty-Fourth Birthday. Oxford: Clarendon Press, 1965. 230-53.

Establishes the courses Boswell attended as a student at the universities of Edinburgh, Glasgow, and Utrecht, and describes their subject matter. At Edinburgh from 1753-1758, Boswell attended the regular public courses in Latin, Greek, logic, natural philosophy, moral philosophy, and mathematics; in addition, he most likely attended private courses in Latin, Greek, and French. For the academic session of 1758-59, Boswell's program included the study of civil law, astronomy, and Roman antiquities. At the University of Glasgow in 1759-60, Boswell attended classes in civil law and Adam Smith's lectures on moral philosophy and rhetoric. At the University of Utrecht during the session of 1763-64, Boswell studied civil law with Professor Christian Heinrich Trotz; French with a master; Greek, Dutch, and geography with friends; and Latin and Scots law by himself. Concludes that Boswell's education was "typical of the education of Scots advocates of family and means in the middle of the eighteenth century."

28. Pottle, Frederick A. James Boswell: The Earlier Years, 1740-1769. New York: McGraw-Hill, 1966.

The first volume of the definitive biography. Contains a detailed and carefully documented account of Boswell's early life--family, education, fits of melancholy, visits to London, the Grand Tour, interviews with Rousseau and Voltaire, involvement with Corsica and Paoli, conflict with his father, intrigues and courtships, practice of the law, and marriage. Includes a description of his juvenilia, an analysis of his motives and methods as a journalist, and a discussion of the composition, reception, and critical achievement of Corsica, "still a very pleasant book," less easy in style than Hebrides and the Life but nevertheless remarkable for its youthful charm and Plutarchian portrait of Paoli.

29. Cole, Richard C. "James Boswell's Irish Cousins." Genealogists' Magazine 16.3 (1969): 81-87.

Traces the genealogical relationship between Boswell and the Montgomeries and his connection with the families of McBride, Boyd, Laing, and Cochrane.

30. Ober, William B. "Boswell's Gonorrhea." Bulletin of the New York Academy of Medicine 45.6 (1969): 587-636. Reprint. "Boswell's Clap." Boswell's Clap and Other Essays: Medical Analyses of Literary Men's Afflictions. Carbondale: Southern Illinois University Press, 1979. 1-39.

Documents Boswell's nineteen episodes of urethral disease, diagnosing twelve as new primary cases of gonorrhea and attributing his death to complications of that disease. Speculates that the unconscious motivation of Boswell's compulsive sexual activity with prostitutes was a desire to demonstrate a disregard for his father's standards, to reassure himself of his masculinity, and to seek the risk of punishment for his sexual transgressions.

31. Foster, Mary Jo. "Margaret Montgomerie: Her Influence on the Life and Writing of James Boswell." Dissertation, Florida State University, 1971.

Examines the relationship between Boswell and his wife, Margaret Montgomerie, who encouraged his writing and remained dedicated to him despite his excesses.

32. Hyde, Mary. "The Impossible Friendship." Harvard Library Bulletin 20 (1972): 5-37, 188-221, 270-317, 372-429. Reprint. The Impossible Friendship: Boswell and Mrs. Thrale. Cambridge: Harvard University Press, 1972.

Provides a year-by-year account of Boswell's relationship with Thrale under four headings: Rivalry (1763-1775), Restraint (1776-1781), Estrangement (1782-1786), and Enmity (1787-1791).

33. Nicholls, Graham. Boswell and Johnson: The Story of a Friendship. Lichfield: James Redshaw, 1976.

Sketches for the non-specialist reader the friendship of Boswell and Johnson, from their initial meeting in Davies's bookshop through their spring visits in London and journey to the Hebrides to Boswell's last gesture of friendship, the writing of the Life.

34. Brady, Frank. James Boswell: The Later Years, 1769-1795. New York: McGraw-Hill, 1984.

Concludes Pottle's definitive life and contains, in addition to the biographical narrative, critical discussions of Boswell as essayist, journalist, and biographer. Describes Boswell's collaboration with Malone on the Hebrides and remarks what makes it "so wonderfully readable": its candor, the range and variety of topics considered, the wealth of detail. Calls attention to the narrative structure--the movement from civilization to the primitive and back again--to Boswell's dual role of participant and reporter, to the interplay of "ordered selectivity" and the "rich randomness of experience"--the combination of art and authenticity. Considers the Life as the uniting of the ethical and anecdotal traditions in biography on an epic scale; describes the making of the Life and praises its presentation of Johnson--dense, complex, human. Analyzes the crucial distinction between Boswell as author and as character and reviews the Life's critical reception.

35. Finlayson, Iain. The Moth and the Candle: A Life of James Boswell. New York: St. Martin's Press, 1984.

Portrays Boswell as a man "convinced that he was fit for nothing," his life--with the exception of the writing of the Life, his one realized ambition--a masochistic enactment of his own unworthiness: "Boswell, time and time again, came back off the ropes for a further dose of punishment."

36. Pottle, Frederick A. "The Literary Career of James Boswell to 1785." Dissertation, Yale University, 1925.

See Item 37.

37. Pottle, Frederick A. The Literary Career of James Boswell, Esq.; Being the Bibliographical Materials for a Life of Boswell. Oxford: Clarendon Press, 1929.

Includes Memoirs of James Boswell, Esq., written by Boswell himself and published in The European Magazine and London Review in 1791, Boswell's only account of his publications. Lists and describes all of Boswell's publications in prose and verse in seven parts: Books, Pamphlets, Broadsides; Periodical Publications; Posthumous Publications; A Doubtful Work (A View of the Edinburgh Theatre during the Summer Season, 1759); Works Attributed to Boswell Wrongly or with Insufficient Evidence; Projected Works; Contemporary Reviews of Boswell's Works.

38. Pottle, Frederick A., and Marion S. Pottle. Catalogue of an Exhibition of the Private Papers of James Boswell from Malahide Castle. New York: Grolier Club, 1930.

Lists and describes Boswell's private papers under four headings: Journals; Letters; Manuscripts; and Books, Broadsides, and Prints.

39. Pottle, Frederick A., and Marion S. Pottle. The Private Papers of James Boswell from Malahide Castle . . . : A Catalogue. London: Oxford University Press, 1931.

Reprints Item 38 with a preface and thirty-one new items listed in an appendix.

40. Abbott, Claude C. A Catalogue of Papers Relating to Boswell, Johnson, and Sir William Forbes, Found at Fettercairn House, A Residence of the Right Honourable Lord Clinton, 1930-1931. Oxford: Clarendon Press, 1936.

Numbers and summarizes papers found at Fettercairn House under ten headings: Letters to Boswell; Drafts of Copies of Letters from Boswell; Letters from Boswell to Sir William Forbes; Seven Major Boswell Manuscripts (journals, registers of letters, notes for a projected life of General Oglethorpe, an account of the last interview with Hume); Miscellaneous Minor Manuscripts in

Boswell's Hand; Letters to Mrs. Boswell; Miscellaneous; Newspaper Cuttings and Pamphlets; Letters from Johnson to Various Correspondents; Johnsoniana.

41. Brown, Anthony E. "Boswellian Studies: A Bibliography." Cairo Studies in English (1963-66). 1-75.

    Lists editions, biographies, bibliographies, and critical studies published between 1763 and 1963.

42. Clifford, James L. and Donald J. Greene. "Boswell (Works and Events Connected with Johnson)." Samuel Johnson: A Survey and Bibliography of Critical Studies. Minneapolis: University of Minnesota Press, 1970. 74-90.

    Includes more than two hundred items, subdivided as Bibliography, Writings, and Commentary.

43. Brown, Anthony E. Boswellian Studies. Hamden, CT: Archon, 1972.

    Updates, revises, and expands Item 41.

44. Glock, Waldo Sumner. "James Boswell." Eighteenth-Century English Literary Studies: A Bibliography. Metuchen, NJ, and London: Scarecrow, 1984.

    Contains approximately one hundred annotated entries for critical articles and books published in the twentieth century.

45. Greene, Donald J. and John A. Vance, eds. A Bibliography of Johnsonian Studies, 1970-1985. English Literary Studies 39. Victoria, British Columbia, Canada: University of Victoria, 1987. 14-22.

    Includes nearly one hundred editions, books, and articles published between 1968 and 1986.

46. Bettany, Lewis. "The Making of Boswell's `Johnson.'" Times Literary Supplement, 13 Feb. 1930: 122.

Calls attention to the correspondence of Temple and Forbes regarding Boswell's literary remains.

47. Chapman, R.W. "Boswell's Archives." Essays and Studies by Members of the English Association. Vol. 17. Oxford: Clarendon Press, 1932. 33-43.

Examines Boswell's will and the correspondence among his executors and descendants concerning the distribution and possible publication of his private papers. Speculates that in 1785 when Boswell discussed in his will the publication of manuscripts, he was thinking only of Johnsonian material--what eventually was published as Hebrides and the Life--not the complete journal.

48. Gray, W. Forbes. "New Light on James Boswell." Juridical Review 50 (1938): 142-64.

Reviews the discovery of documents at Fettercairn House--letters to Boswell from various correspondents and from him to Forbes--and summarizes what they reveal about Boswell's domestic relationships, his friendships with Dalrymple and Forbes, his legal career, and his opinions on contemporary political events.

49. Pottle, Frederick A., Joseph Foladare, John D. Kirby, et al. Index to the Private Papers of James Boswell from the Malahide Castle in the Collection of Lieutenant Colonel Ralph Heyward Isham. New York: N.p., 1938.

Provides a complete index of Scott and Pottle's edition of Boswell's private papers.

50. Roberts, S.C. "The Discovery of James Boswell." Discovery, n.s. 1 (Aug. 1938): 252-54.

Outlines the events leading to the discovery of the Boswell papers at Malahide Castle and Fettercairn House.

51. Morley, Edith J. "Boswell in Light of Recent Discoveries." Quarterly Review 272 (Jan. 1939): 77-93.

Describes the contents of Scott and Pottle's edition of the private papers, concluding that only after carefully studying these new materials can one truly appreciate Boswell's astounding literary achievement.

52. "The Malahide and Fettercairn Papers." Times Literary Supplement, 18 Dec. 1948: 270.

Speculates on the disposition of the Boswell collection.

53. Abbott, Claude C. "New Light on Johnson and Boswell." The Listener, 19 May 1949: 853-54.

Sketches the discovery and publication of Boswell's papers and concludes "the ghosts of Auchinleck should now be fully appeased."

54. Altick, Richard D. "The Secret of the Ebony Cabinet." The Scholar Adventurers. New York: Macmillan, 1950. 16-36.

In a casebook describing successes of literary research, retells the story of the discovery of Boswell's papers: Major Stone's finding one of Boswell's letters used as wrapping paper in Boulogne in 1850; Tinker's locating and Lt. Col. Isham's purchasing the papers at Malahide Castle; Abbott's discovery at Fettercairn house of still more paper; and Yale University's eventual acquisition of the entire remaining Boswell archive--journals, thousands of letters to and from Boswell, manuscripts of Hebrides and the Life. Notes how these documents led to a complete reevaluation of Boswell's character and biographical method, proving--as Boswell himself so fervently believed--that he was "a man worthy of permanent fame--not notoriety--for his own sake."

55. Basso, Hamilton. "The Boswell Detective Story." Life, 4 Dec. 1950: 93-104.

Provides an illustrated account of the "improbable and incredible" discovery of Boswell's papers from Major Stone's purchase of a letter in Boulogne in 1850 to the acquisition by Yale of more than four thousand items in 1949.

56. Morley, Christopher. "The Boswell Papers: A Legend of Impropriety." Saturday Review, 7 Oct. 1950: 11-14. Reprint. Preface. Boswell's London Journal, 1762-1763. Now First Published from the Original Manuscript. Edited by Frederick A. Pottle. New York: McGraw-Hill, 1950. ix-xxix.

Tells for a general audience an abridged version of the history of the Boswell papers, emphasizing the patient work of dedicated scholars and collectors--Tinker, A. Edward Newton, Lt. Col. Isham, and Abbott.

57. Fadiman, Clifton. "Party of One." Holiday 16 (Aug. 1954): 6-8.

Places Boswell among those writers who have gained literary fame only after their deaths--Donne, Hopkins, Kierkegaard--and recounts the discovery of Boswell's papers in the form of a three-act drama.

58. Buchanan, David. The Treasure of Auchinleck: The Story of the Boswell Papers. New York: McGraw-Hill, 1974.

Provides a detailed, carefully documented, and complex history of the Boswell papers, from "the legend of destruction" through the inquiries, searches, discoveries, and negotiations of Tinker, Lt. Col. Isham, Scott, and Abbott to the acquisition and editing of the archives by Yale University. Includes appendices describing more recent acquisitions of Boswellian material, Boswell's correspondence with Johnson, the manuscript of the Life, missing leaves from Boswell's journals (those presumably recounting his affair with Therese Le Vasseur), papers from the Isham Collection not at Yale, and a missing manuscript--Boswell's Address to the Signet Library, Edinburgh.

59. Hyde, Mary. "Boswell's Ebony Cabinet." Studies in the Eighteenth Century III: Papers Presented at the Third David Nichol Smith Memorial Seminar, Canberra, 1973. Toronto: University of Toronto Press, 1976. 21-35.

Seeks to dispel the myth that "the ebony cabinet is synonymous with the `papers of James Boswell'" by showing that much of the manuscript material was placed there only shortly before it was examined in the 1920s by Tinker and Lt. Col. Isham and by reviewing how much material--the manuscript of Hebrides, for example--was discovered elsewhere on the Talbot's Malahide estate.

60. Greene, Donald J. "A Bear by the Tail: The Genesis of the Boswell Industry." Studies in Burke and His Time 18 (1977): 114-27.

Reviews favorably Item 58, calling it a masterpiece, a complex and fascinating detective story. Claims the Boswell papers themselves are of little literary value, that there is little interest in "the details of the day-to-day existence of a neurotic and not very successful Scottish lawyer and literary dabbler."

61. Pottle, Frederick A. Pride and Negligence: The History of the Boswell Papers. New York: McGraw-Hill, 1982.

Revises a twenty-year-old unpublished narrative of the Boswell papers, incorporating new evidence and supplementing it with epilogues describing Yale's acquisition of papers since 1950 and the history of the publication of the Boswell papers.

62. Hyde, Mary. "Adam, Tinker, and Newton." Johnson and His Age. Edited by James Engell. Cambridge: Harvard University Press, 1984. 285-307.

Draws on private correspondence to trace the activities between 1909 and 1929--collecting, cataloguing, and editing of rare manuscripts, including Boswell's letters and proof sheets of the Life--of three eminent Johnsonians and Boswellians: Tinker, Yale professor of English; R.B. Adam II, president of a department store in Buffalo, New York, and an avid book collector; and A. Edward Newton, a Philadelphia businessman, author, and collector.

Life of Johnson

63. Sillard, P.A. "The Prince of Biographers." Atlantic Monthly, Aug. 1901: 213-21.

Attributes the unmatched success of the Life to Boswell's fascination with human character, his gift for friendship, and his "capacity to take pains."

64. Chesterton, G.K. "Boswell's `Johnson.'" Good Words 44 (1903): 774-77.

Justifies an abridgement of the Life by arguing that, unedited, the book intimidates readers and by noting that our knowledge of other great figures such as Jesus Christ and Socrates is in fact drawn from fragmentary documents. Considers Boswell one of the great men of the eighteenth century, and the Life "a great triumph of psychological analysis."

65. Birrell, Augustine. "Boswell as Biographer." In the Name of the Bodleian and Other Essays. New York: Charles Scribner's Sons, 1905. 133-39. London: Elliot and Stock, 1905. 91-95. Reprint. Collected Essays and Addresses, 1880-1920, vol. 1. London: J.M. Dent, 1922. 150-54.

Reviews Macaulay's and Carlyle's descriptions of Boswell as a coxcomb and a hero-worshipper and suggests that neither properly acknowledges the conscious nature of his artistry.

66. Raleigh, Sir Walter. "Johnson without Boswell." Six Essays on Johnson. London: Oxford University Press, 1910. 40-74.

Reviews early biographies by Hawkins, Thrale, Murphy, and others to determine just how faithful Boswell's account of Johnson's life and character is. Concludes that Boswell does indeed have limitations and blind spots--for example, his unfair portrayal of Goldsmith and his inability to portray Johnson's lighter side--but that Boswell is remarkably accurate: he occasionally exaggerates but never invents or suppresses; the main outlines of Boswell's Johnson are confirmed and preserved in a number of other sources. Suggests that Boswell did not "make" Johnson: he is simply his most gifted, most devoted, and most affectionate biographer.

67. "Boswell and Goldsmith." Outlook 97 (1911): 580-81.

Claims that Boswell failed to understand Goldsmith and to appreciate his wit and charm, and suggests that Boswell's depiction of him in the Life is maliciously distorted.

68. Fitzgerald, Percy. "Boswell's Autobiography." Quarterly Review 214 (1911): 24-44.

Argues that Boswell's true purpose in writing the Life was not to preserve and illuminate Johnson's character but to "furnish a complete and favourable account of himself." Suggests that Boswell revised conversations in order to gratify his own vanity and slyly diminishes Johnson so as to make himself appear to be a greater man by comparison.

69. Lee, Sir Sidney. Principles of Biography. The Leslie Stephen Lecture. Cambridge: Cambridge University Press, 1911. 42-49.

Considers the Life as the best biography in any language and attributes its power to "a singular union of two exceptional human forces": Johnson, "a being of rare intellectual and moral manliness," and Boswell, his industrious, faithful, and candid chronicler.

70. Fitch, George Hamlin. "Old Dr. Johnson and His Boswell." Comfort Found in Good Old Books. San Francisco: Paul Elder, 1911. 116-23.

Calls the Life "one of the great books of the world," old-fashioned in style but "very modern in spirit."

71. Fitzgerald, Percy. Boswell's Autobiography. London: Chatto and Windus, 1912.

Claims that Boswell's true purpose in writing about Johnson was to record his own accomplishments and to enhance his own reputation: the Life is in fact not Johnson's biography but Boswell's autobiography, an account of his life, character, and opinions, Boswell's chief aim being "his own advancement and self-exaltation." Suggests that Boswell attempts to portray himself as superior by subtly "levelling down" Johnson: he minimizes his achievements, criticizes his opinions, and presents him in unflattering situations. Believes that after enduring years of Johnson's tyrannical and insulting treatment, Boswell quarreled with him months before his death and that Boswell's resentment and animosity are evident throughout the Life, especially in his treatment of Johnson's death, seemingly a respectful, judicious account but really a "sharp, bitter attack" on Johnson's moral character.

72. Harrison, Frederic. "Great Biographies." Among My Books. London: Macmillan, 1912. 65-85.

Implores readers to return to Plutarch and Boswell, authors too often studied in one's early days and then forgotten.

73. Johnson, Lionel P. Post Liminium: Essays and Critical Papers. Edited by Thomas Whittemore. New York: Mitchell Kennerly, 1912. 136-42.

Praises Boswell's "invincible vivacity": his insatiable curiosity, his desire for new sensation, his love for the "piquant reality" he preserves in the Life.

74. "Whoever Will Write a Life." Public Opinion, 10 May 1912: 452.

Notes the irony of the fact that Mason's Life of Gray, a book Johnson found "mightily dull," served as Boswell's model for the Life.

75. Newmark, Leo. "News for Bibliophiles." Nation, 11 Sept. 1913: 232.

Calls attention to an eighteenth-century German translation of the Life.

76. Ralli, Augustus. "Boswell." Westminster Review 179 (1913): 270-83.

Argues that prejudice has hindered a just appreciation of Boswell's literary achievement and his character: the Life is "no mere transcript of reality" but rather a work of imagination. Plagued by the "emotional instability of the man of genius," Boswell possessed a poetic temperament, which left him ill-equipped for the world of business but was the source of the powerful feeling and command of metaphor evident in the Life.

77. Nicoll, W. Robertson. "The Six Best Biographies." A Bookman's Letters. London: Hodder and Stoughton, 1915. 17-25.

Defines the prerequisites of a great biography--a truly great subject, special materials, an artistic biographer--and places the Life at the top of the list of the greatest lives--Lockhart's Scott, Gaskell's Charlotte Bronte, Trevelyan's Macaulay, Froude's Carlyle, and Morley's Gladstone.

78. Tinker, Chauncey B. "Boswell and the Art of Intimate Biography." The Salon and English Letters: Chapters on the Interpretations of Literature and Society in the Age of Johnson. New York: Macmillan, 1915. 268-84.

Reviews the reception of Boswell's Hebrides and Life to illustrate how alarming contemporaries found the frank and detailed method he learned from Johnson. Argues that Boswell surpasses all previous biographical endeavors--table talk, eulogy, anecdote, ana, memoir--and achieves something completely new, the perfection of intimate biography, remarkably complete, accurate, and vivid in its rendering of the social world.

79. Dunn, Waldo H. English Biography. New York: E.P. Dutton and Co., 1916. 112-29.

Considers the Life the zenith of English biography, "that work toward which all English biography before 1791 tends, and to which all since that date looks back reminiscently." Believes Boswell's contribution to the development of the genre was his combining methods, none original, practiced previously by Walton, Roper, Aubrey, Mason, and Johnson: the inclusion of letters, conversation, anecdotes, domestic details.

80. Saintsbury, George. "Johnson, Boswell, and Goldsmith." The Peace of the Augustans. London: George Bell and Sons, 1916. 177-212.

Asserts that Boswell "was a great artist" and his biographical writing an "astounding mirror" of his age.

81. Gardiner, Alfred G. "On Boswell and His Miracle." Pebbles on the Shore. New York: E.P. Dutton and Co., 1917. 62-66.

Describes Boswell as uncouth, childish, lacking in self-respect and humor, doglike in his devotion to Johnson, and claims that these qualities enabled him to write the Life, an inexhaustible masterpiece, far more engaging than anything written by Johnson.

82. Newton, A. Edward. "James Boswell--His Book." The Amenities of Book-Collecting and Kindred Affections. Boston: Atlantic Monthly Press, 1918. 145-85. Excerpt reprinted in Item 216.

Blames Macaulay for obscuring "the real Samuel Johnson and the real James Boswell," each a genius in his own right: Johnson, the greatest of subjects, his own astonishing creation, and Boswell, the world's greatest portrait painter, who made Johnson available to generations of readers.

83. Russell, A.J. "An Unpardonable Interruption." Bellman 24 (1918): 664-65.

Recalls Boswell's description in the Life of taking tea with Fanny Burney on 26 May 1783, and speculates that on this occasion, Johnson found Boswell's presence unwelcome.

84. Roberts, S.C. The Story of Doctor Johnson, Being an Introduction to Boswell's Life. Cambridge: Cambridge University Press, 1919.

Tells a "simpler form" of the story of Johnson's life--with extracts from Boswell, Thrale, and Fanny Burney--in the hopes of enhancing the appreciation of new readers of the Life.

85. Cross, Wilbur L. "An Outline of Biography from Plutarch to Strachey." Yale Review 11 (Oct. 1921): 140-57. Reprint. An Outline of Biography from Plutarch to Strachey. New York: Henry Holt and Co., 1924.

Calls the Life "the most complete portrait of a man ever put into words" and attributes its power to the conjunction of a great and fascinating subject and a devoted and perceptive biographer.

86. Mais, S.P.B. "James Boswell." Why We Should Read--. London: Richards, 1921. 35-37.

Recommends the Life as a book "to be opened at random while waiting for a train or a doctor or a dentist" and praises Boswell's ability to portray Johnson's complex character: pious and superstitious, sociable and melancholy, sluggish by nature, yet capable of tremendous labor.

87. Osgood, Charles G. Introduction. The R.B. Adam Library Relating to Dr. Samuel Johnson and His Era. 3 vols. Buffalo, NY: Privately printed, 1921. i-viii.

Calls special attention to those materials in the collection which shed light on Boswell's artistry: a notebook which Boswell kept during his visit with Johnson to Oxford, Birmingham, Lichfield, and Ashbourne in 1776, and a portion of the manuscript of the Life.

88. Smith, Minna Steele. "Manuscript Notes by Madame Piozzi in a Copy of Boswell's Life of Johnson." London Mercury 5 (1922): 286-93. Reprint. Living Age, 4 Mar. 1922: 536-42.

Examines and excerpts Piozzi's marginal notes in two copies of the Life, dated 1807 and 1817. She defends herself against Boswell's charges of inaccuracy, identifies a number of unnamed friends and acquaintances, and adds her own details to Boswell's anecdotes.

89. Tinker, Chauncey B. "The Magnum Opus." Atlantic Monthly, Mar. 1922: 356-61. Reprint. Item 6. Excerpt reprinted in Item 216.

Assembles quotations from Boswell's letter describing his biographical method and examines revisions in the proofsheets of the Life in order to show that it is the product of conscious artistry, that Boswell's effects are calculated.

90. Chapman, R.W. "Birkbeck Hill's Johnson." Times Literary Supplement, 26 July 1923: 504.

Suggests how errors in Hill might be eliminated in a new edition.

91. Saintsbury, George. "Some Great Biographies." Essays in English Literature, 1875-1920. London: J.M. Dent, 1923. 412-16.

Considers the Life as an example of "mixed" biography, combining letters and narrative. Argues that this method, apparently easy, is in fact extraordinarily difficult to employ skillfully: few of Boswell's modern imitators, for example, share his gift for keeping his subject always in view, for including no superfluous detail.

92. Canby, Henry S. "Boswell's `Johnson.'" Definitions, Essays in Contemporary Criticism. 2nd Series. New York: Harcourt, Brace and Company, 1924. 249-53.

Reviews a new edition of the Life by remarking that despite the remoteness of the eighteenth-century world--its secure social order, its religious certainty--modern readers would do well to imitate the strength of Johnson's character: his tolerance, his greatness of mind, his devotion to truth.

93. "Proofsheets of Boswell's Johnson." Times Literary Supplement, 17 Jan. 1924: 44.

Announces the publication of R.B. Adam's facsimile.

94. Collins, Joseph. The Doctor Looks at Biography. New York: Doubleday Doran, 1925. 25ff.

Describes the Life as "the most perfect portrait of a man ever painted with words," the standard for intimate biography.

95. Gissing, A. "Appleby School: An Extra-Illustration to Boswell." Cornhill Magazine 133 (Apr. 1926): 404-14.

Supplements Boswell's account of Johnson's attempt to become master of a school in Leicestershire.

96. Pocock, G.N. "The Lexicographer's Chair." Little Room. New York: Dutton, 1926. 102-9.

Praises the Life as "a miracle of a book," the product of Boswell's "almost Shakespearian" genius.

97. Russell, Sir Charles. "Johnson, Gibbon, and Boswell." Fortnightly Review, May 1926: 629-35.

Speculates that "the coldness" between Johnson and Gibbon was caused in part by Boswell's ill will toward Gibbon, whose literary success he envied.

98. Chapman, R.W. "Boswell's Proof-Sheets." London Mercury, Nov. 1926: 50-58; Dec. 1926: 171-80.

Prints marginal comments made by Boswell, his printer, and Malone on the proofs of the Life and describes their corrections, alterations, and cancels.

99. Bennett, James O. "Boswell's Life of Johnson." Much Loved Books: Best Sellers of the Ages. New York: Boni and Liveright, 1927. 197-203.

Praises the Life as a valuable record of Johnson's wise and witty conversation, a faithful record of a fascinating life, and a lively picture of the age.

100. Gordon, George. "Boswell's Life of Johnson." Companionable Books, 1927. Reprint. Freeport, New York: Books for Libraries Press, 1968. 45-53. More Companionable Books. London: Chatto and Windus, 1947. 31-36.

Attributes the increasing popularity of the Life among the disillusioned readers of the early twentieth century to Johnson's "majestic common sense" and his refusal to pretend that "life can yield more than we are willing to put into it, or that Utopia can be reached by exhalations of the breath."

101. "How Many Issues Are There of the First Edition of Boswell's Life of Johnson?" Bulletin of the New York Public Library 31 (1927): 826-27.

Suggests that there may have been three issues of the first edition of the Life rather than two, as book collectors previously had assumed.

102. Johnston, James C. Biography: The Literature of Personality. New York: Century Co., 1927.

Claims that the Life remains the standard for modern objective biography and describes Boswell's unique combination of correspondence, anecdote, and conversation.

103. Bolton, John H. A Commentary and Questionnaire on Selections from Boswell's Life of Johnson. London: Sir I. Pitman and Sons, 1928.

Provides an introduction to the Life for students.

104. Chapman, R.W. "Boswell's Revises of the Life of Johnson." Johnson and Boswell Revised by Themselves and Others. Oxford: Clarendon Press, 1928. 21-50.

Describes the revised proofs of the first edition of the Life and lists Boswell's marginalia in four categories: instructions to the printer; corrections; alteration of Johnson's words; and the suppression by means of cancel leaves of certain passages and names.

105. Nicolson, Harold. "The Boswell Formula, 1791." The Development of English Biography. New York: Harcourt, Brace and Co., 1928. 87-109. Reprint. Item 216.

Attempts to determine the literary value of the Life by first dismissing "accidental" circumstances, Boswell's charm and his good fortune to write about so engaging a figure as Johnson. Claims that Boswell lacks genius but possesses a pleasant style, a talent for dramatization, and amazing powers of observation. Suggests that Boswell's originality consists of his self-conscious fusing of biographical conventions and methods employed earlier by Johnson, Mason, and the writers of ana.

106. Powell, Lawrence F. "The Revision of Dr. Birkbeck Hill's Boswell." Johnson and Boswell Revised by Themselves and Others. Oxford: Clarendon Press, 1928. 53-66.

Explains why Hill's edition of the Life needs revising: the third edition, chosen by Hill as the copy text, is full of errors and must be corrected by discovering the best readings--whether in the first, second, or third editions--by noting variants, and by correcting Boswell's own textual errors. In addition, newly discovered diaries, letters, and manuscripts, unknown to Hill, provide information that must be incorporated into the commentary.

107. Buxton, Charles Roden. "Boswell's Life of Johnson." A Politician Plays Truant. London: Christopher, 1929. 83-99.

Enumerates those qualities of Johnson's mind and character, which, without the Life, would be unknown: his courage, generosity, humor, and vast learning.

108. "Notes on Sales: Boswell and Shakespeare Problems." Times Literary Supplement, 16 May 1929: 408.

Calls attention to the existence of at least one copy of the first edition of the Life with cancelled matter printed as Boswell had originally written and passed it in proof form.

109. Scott, Geoffrey. ed. The Making of the Life of Johnson as Shown in Boswell's First Notes. Vol. 6 of The Private Papers of James Boswell from Malahide Castle in the Collection of Lieutenant Colonel Ralph Heyward Isham. Edited by Geoffrey Scott and Frederick A. Pottle. Mt. Vernon, NY: Privately printed, 1929. Reprint. Item 216.

Describes and provides examples of materials relating to the making of the Life: shorthand notes, nearly contemporary with the events described, used as an aid in bringing up the journal and then discarded; papers apart, loose sheets covered with memoranda dealing with isolated incidents, miscellaneous notebooks containing conversations and anecdotes; the journals, the continuous narrative of Boswell's life. Explains and illustrates Boswell's composition process--sorting, classifying, selecting, and rewriting--as he revised the journals through a rough draft, a revised draft, and the first edition.

110. Ward, H. Gordon. "A Spanish Quotation in Boswell's Johnson." Notes and Queries 156 (1929): 111-12.

Identifies the source of Owen Cambridge's quotation from "a Spanish writer" on 9 April 1778 as Quevedo's sonnet addressed to Rome buried in its ruins.

111. Fortescue-Brickdale, Charles. "Dr. Johnson and Mrs. Macaulay: The Credibility of Boswell." Notes and Queries 159 (1930): 111-12.

Examines Johnson's account, reported by Boswell in the Life, of his suggesting to Catharine Macaulay that if she believed in equality so strongly as she professed, she ought to invite her footman to dine with her. Compares Johnson's account with Macaulay's slightly different version published in her Letters on Education (1790) and concludes that hers is the more "natural and probable."

112. Inge, Charles C. "The Making of Boswell's Johnson." Times Literary Supplement, 6 Feb. 1930: 85-86.

Summarizes Scott's analysis of Boswell's biographical method.

113. Metcalf, John Calvin. The Stream of English Biography. New York: The Century Co., 1930. 21-26, 119-20.

Introduces a selection of passages from the Life by praising Boswell's "extraordinary" industry and "phenomenal" memory and by describing the Life not merely as a miscellany of brilliant conversations and anecdotes but as a well-constructed whole, exhibiting "the detailed diversity and the larger unity of a Gothic cathedral."

114. Pearson, Hesketh. Ventilations: Being Biographical Asides. London and Philadelphia: J.B. Lippincott Co., 1930. 11-20, 37-48.

Proposes that Boswell be treated not as a master of biographical accuracy--his portrait of Goldsmith is only one example of his partiality and distortion--but as a great imaginative artist, whose Johnson, like Shakespeare's Falstaff, is a memorable dramatic creation.

115. Gow, A.S.F. "The Unknown Johnson." Life and Letters, Sept. 1931: 200-215. Reprint. Item 216.

Calls attention to limitations in Boswell's portrait of Johnson: Boswell knew little of Johnson's first fifty-four years, which occupy less than a third of the Life; and he did not fully appreciate or portray important traits of Johnson's character, his boisterous, irrational laughter, for example, or his affection for women, by turns fatherly, gallant, charming, and grotesque. Concludes, however, that Boswell's portrait "is not the less true because some of the features are in shadow."

116. Longaker, Mark. "Boswell's Life of Johnson." English Biography of the Eighteenth Century. Philadephia: University of Pennsylvania Press, 1931. 407-76.

Characterizes the Life as the finest biography ever written, a product of the spirit of the age, and the culmination of the century's interest in lives, memoirs, correspondence, and anecdote. Enumerates the character traits that made Boswell a good companion and a good biographer--sociability, sincerity, aggressiveness, inquisitiveness--and describes Boswell's method of recording Johnson's conversations. Reviews Boswell's theory of biography and the reception and reputation of the Life.

117. Blunden, Edmund. "A Boswellian Error." Votive Tablets; Studies Chiefly Appreciative of English Authors and Books. New York: Harper and Bros., 1932. 160-62.

Calls attention to the claim of Elizabeth Le Noir, the daughter of Christopher Smart, that she--not a Miss Hunter, as Boswell states--was the young girl who asked, "Pray, Dr. Johnson, why do you make such strange gestures?" Includes anecdotes from her writings concerning Johnson, Goldsmith, and Smart.

118. Elovson, Harald. "`Mr. Kristrom' in Boswell's Life of Dr. Johnson." Modern Language Review 27 (1932): 210-12.

Identifies the Mr. Kristom mentioned by Boswell as Pehr Christom, a Swedish philologist who lived in London as a pensioned tutor.

119. Reilly, Joseph J. "Bozzy: The Man Who Made Johnson." Dear Prue's Husband. New York: Macmillan, 1932. 68-78.

Describes Boswell as misunderstood--by his wife, by Macaulay, by Carlyle. His curiosity, "everlastingly trying to peer into other men's minds"; his considerable intelligence; his method of directing, remembering, and recording conversation--these, too often obscured by Boswell's silliness and immaturity, account for the greatness of the Life.

120. Willing-Denton, E.K. "Boswell and the Copyright of the Life." Times Literary Supplement, 1 Dec. 1932: 923.

Argues that Boswell printed and published the Letter to Lord Chesterfield and Conversation with George III as separate pamphlets prior to the publication of the Life at least in part to secure his literary property.

121. Pottle, Frederick A. "The New Birkbeck Hill." Times Literary Supplement, 3 Aug. 1933: 525.

Presents eleven queries concerning the fourth volume of Hill's edition of the Life.

122. Rait, Sir Robert. "Boswell and Lockhart." Essays by Divers Hands 12 (1933): 105-27.

Compares the biographical methods of Boswell and Lockhart: both relied on letters and well-selected details to create truthful, balanced portraits of their subjects, although Lockhart departed from Boswell's model by choosing not to include conversations and by altering the text of Sir Walter Scott's letters.

123. Chapman, R.W. "Hill's Boswell." Saturday Review of Literature, 23 Mar. 1935: 564.

Defends the decision to revise Hill's edition of the Life rather than to produce a new variorum edition.

124. Smith-Dampier, J.L. Who's Who in Boswell? Oxford: Shakespeare Head Press, 1935.

Contains 365 one-page essays on Johnson and lives of the dramatis personae of the Life.

125. Britt, Albert. "Johnson and Boswell." The Great Biographers. New York: Whittlesey House, 1936. 67-76.

Considers the Life "the focal point of English biography," a work which, along with Johnson's Lives of the Poets and Mason's Life of Gray, brought new dignity to the writing profession.

126. Clifford, James L. "Further Letters of the Johnson Circle." Bulletin of the John Rylands Library 20 (1936): 268-85.

Describes a collection of Piozzi's papers acquired by the John Rylands Library, including several letters that shed light on her rivalry with Boswell: letters from Samuel Lyson to her in Italy keeping her abreast of Boswell's research, correspondence with Anna Seward about the acquisition of Johnson's letters.

127. Cowie, Alexander. "A Boswell Misquotation." Times Literary Supplement, 25 Apr. 1936: 356.

Corrects a misquotation from the Life which Stevenson affixed to his "Apology for Idlers."

128. Johnson, Edgar. "Eighteenth-Century Apogee." One Mighty Torrent: The Drama of Biography. New York: Stackpole Sons, 1937; Macmillan, 1955. 217-33.

Asserts that Boswell's Life is not the result of luck but of "forethought, labor, and amazing skill." Outlines the character of Boswell's Johnson: a Tory, a devout member of the Church of England, a man subject to melancholy but with a tremendous zest for living. Praises Boswell for his ability to create "the illusion of actual presence and movement," for his dramatic skill, and for his handling of Johnson's early years despite the paucity of his materials.

129. Harazti, Zoltan. "The Life of Johnson." More Books: The Bulletin of the Boston Public Library 13 (1938): 99-112.

Describes a first edition of the Life acquired by the Boston Public Library and reviews what the Malahide Papers reveal about Boswell's plan, progress, and revision, noting that the manuscripts corroborate his statements about Malone's role--he was an advisor only, not a co-author.

130. Morley, Christopher. "A Supper of Larks." Saturday Review of Literature, 3 Dec. 1938: 13, 26.

Reviews Piozzi's marginal notes in two copies of the Life.

131. Walcutt, Charles C. "Captain Marryat and Boswell's Life of Johnson." Notes and Queries 174 (1938): 27-28.

Suggests that Frederick Marryat's novel Peter Simple (1833) contains an anecdote borrowed from the Life.

132. Chapman, R.W. "Dr. Johnson's Letters: Notes on Boswell's Texts." Times Literary Supplement, 25 Feb. 1939: 128; 4 March 1939: 140.

Concludes, based on the collation of Boswell's versions of Johnson's letters with a small number of originals, that Boswell's text is "remarkably good for his time."

133. H., O.N. "Boswell's Life of Johnson: Translations." Notes and Queries 177 (1939): 351.

Asks for information on translations of the Life.

134. Bennett, Charles H. "A Boswell Reference." Times Literary Supplement, 18 May 1940: 248.

Identifies the source of an anecdote in the Life concerning Beaumont and Fletcher.

135. Phelps, William Lyon. "Esquire's Five-Minute Shelf." Esquire Sept. 1940: 170-171. Reprint. Item 216.

Recommends the Life because it is an excellent "bed book" and because it is a book "exclusively for adult readers."

136. Pottle, Frederick A. "Boswell's Life of Johnson: Translations." Notes and Queries 178 (1940): 50-51.

Replies to Item 133. Finds no complete translations of the Life and three partial translations--in German, Russian, and Swedish.

137. Wilson, F.P. "Table Talk." Huntington Library Quarterly 4 (1940): 27-46.

Traces the development of the genre of ana or table talk--collections of "loose thoughts, or casual hints, dropped by eminent men"--and praises Boswell's Life as the most authentic biography ever written and the fullest and most intelligent collection of table talk ever assembled.

138. Dunn, Charles E. "James Boswell and His Book." Advance 133 (1941): 5-6.

Marks the two-hundredth anniversary of Boswell's birth by praising the Life as a lively and humane portrait of an extraordinary man, "of peculiar value to ministers, for it is full of references to church and religion."

139. Pottle, Frederick A. "Queries on Boswell's Johnson." Notes and Queries 181 (1941): 317.

Requests information concerning a number of people mentioned in the Life: Sir John Halkett, John Gainsford Becher or Beecher, Henry Samson Woodfall, Miss Edwards, Lady Phillipina Knight, and the family of John McAdam.

140. R., V. "Johnson, Boswell, and Grattan." Notes and Queries 181 (1941): 273.

Dates and corrects a quotation in the Life from a speech given by Grattan in the Irish House of Commons.

141. Stauffer, Donald A. The Art of Biography in Eighteenth-Century England. 2 vols. New York: Russell and Russell, 1941. 411-55.

Places Boswell among "the great names" of eighteenth-century biography and contradicts the notion that he is simply a recording machine. Praises Boswell for his strict adherence to truth, his skill in reproducing Johnson's conversations, and his dramatic ability. Points out weaknesses in the Life: the style is undistinguished and the structure is faulty--too long and poorly planned.

142. Alger, F. "Boswell's Life of Johnson." Notes and Queries 183 (1942): 141-42.

Responds to Item 145 by providing Charles Bourchier's date of death, 2 March 1810.

143. Andrews, H.C. "Boswell's Life of Johnson." Notes and Queries 182 (1942): 235.

In response to Item 145, locates James Bennet's school and identifies one of his pupils.

144. Pottle, Frederick A., and Charles H. Bennett. "Boswell and Mrs. Piozzi." Modern Philology 39 (1942): 421-30.

Examines the charge made by James Clifford in his Hester Lynch Piozzi (Mrs. Thrale) that Boswell in the Life "deliberately falsified his materials so as to prejudice readers of his Life of Johnson against Mrs. Piozzi." Argues that Boswell, though admittedly biased, "never tampers with historical facts"; agrees with Boswell that Piozzi's own biographical writings were frequently inaccurate.

145. Powell, Lawrence F. "Boswell's Life of Johnson." Notes and Queries 182 (1942): 136, 147, 176, 206, 209, 235, 260; 183 (1942): 17, 141-42; 184 (1943): 46.

Seeks additional information concerning a number of people mentioned in the Life. Identifies Somerset Draper, a bookseller mentioned in the Life.

146. DeCastro, J. Paul. "Laetitia Hawkins and Boswell." Notes and Queries 185 (1943): 373-74.

Calls attention to an entry in Laetitia Hawkins's diary describing Boswell's attempt to obtain Johnson's papers through a scheme involving Francis Barber.

147. Osgood, Charles G. "Lady Phillipina Knight and Her Boswell." Princeton University Library Chronicle 4 (1943): 37-49.

Describes a first edition of the Life in the Princeton library that is filled with Lady Phillipina Knight's anecdotes and reminiscences of the Johnson circle. Notes that Lady Knight considered Boswell impudent, mischievous, and the victim of a "heated imagination."

148. Bailey, John. "The Genius of Boswell." Dr. Johnson and His Circle. London: Williams and Nergate; New York: Henry Holt and Co.,

1913. Revised and edited by Lawrence F. Powell. London: Oxford University Press, 1944. 37-69.

Characterizes the Life as "one of the great books of the world," the product not merely of Boswell's devotion to fact but to his genius--his "imaginative and emotional insight."

149. Juvenis, Miles. "Boswell in Normandy." The Spectator, 1 Sept. 1944: 193.

Recommends Boswell's Life, an inexhaustible source of wisdom, as a book especially well-suited to be read on one's travels.

150. Metzdorf, Robert F. "A New Wordsworth Letter." Modern Language Notes 59 (1944): 168-70.

Calls attention to an unpublished letter from Wordsworth to John Wilson Croker, dated 24 February 1830. Having learned of Croker's forthcoming edition of the Life, Wordsworth forwarded a copy of a note by Sir George Beaumont that describes the pains Boswell took to insure the accuracy of the conversations he reproduced.

151. Chapman, R.W. Two Centuries of Johnsonian Scholarship; Being the Twelfth Lecture on the David Murray Foundation in the University of Glasgow delivered on May 3rd, 1945. Glasgow: Jackson, Son and Co., 1945.

Notes that Boswell, only a fair critic and scholar, was not especially well-suited to the task of establishing the Johnson canon. Believes that modern students owe their greatest debt to Boswell for his preserving and recreating Johnson's life: a man of tremendous vitality and humanity, he remains the greatest of biographers, who did not invent Johnson but "did transform him into something much larger than, without their association, he could ever have become."

152. Pottle, Frederick A. "The Power of Memory in Boswell and Scott." Essays on the Eighteenth Century Presented to David Nichol Smith in Honor of his Seventieth Birthday. Oxford: Clarendon Press, 1945. Reprint. New York: Russell and Russell, 1963. 168-89.

Notes that both Boswell and Sir Walter Scott possessed remarkable memories, though of very different sorts. Boswell's memory is striking for its "wealth of detail," its "circumstantial accuracy"--given the right prompts, he "had something that looks like total recall"--and for its selectivity: his genius is for remembering significant detail. He remembers both accurately and imaginatively and thus presents in the Life an "imaginative reconstruction." Scott's memory, on the other hand, in matters of fact, was often "wildly inaccurate"; he tended to alter details for effect, to construct memorable fictions. In this, Scott is characteristically Romantic, valuing not the facts of ordinary perception but "imaginative recall," the mingling of perception and imagination associated with Wordsworth.

153. Adams, J. Donald. "Speaking of Books." New York Times Book Review, 23 June 1946: 2.

Credits Geoffrey Scott with exploding the myth of Boswell as a mindless transcriber of conversation and with revealing the extent of his conscious artistry in the Life.

154. Carver, George. "Boswell and the Johnson." Alms for Oblivion: Books, Men and Biography. Science and Culture Series. Edited by Edward Dahlberg. Milwaukee: Bruce Publications, 1946. 160-69.

Notes the irony that Boswell, the greatest of biographers, until the discovery of his private papers, had never been adequately treated in a life of his own. Suggests that a satisfactory biography must acknowledge the years of heroic labor that went into the making of the Life. Boswell suffered the death of his wife, failing health, and depressed spirits: "In spite of everything, however, he persevered."

155. Chapman, R.W. "Boswell's Editors." Times Literary Supplement, 14 Sept. 1946: 439.

Calls Hill's edition "deficient in historical method"; he takes the third edition--which Boswell did not live to complete--as definitive.

156. Tucker, William J. "Prince of Biographers." Catholic World 163 (1946): 218-24.

Seeks to defend Boswell against charges that he was a foolish sycophant and notes his loyalty, wit, frankness, and understanding made his acquaintance desired by some of the most eminent men of his day. Maintains that Boswell took notes in Johnson's company and never "polished a conversation," but affirms Boswell's artistry: the Life is among the most entrancing books in literature.

157. Starrett, Vincent. "Boswell and Dr. Johnson." Books and Bipeds. New York: Argus Books, 1947. 200-202.

Claims that "if Johnson is great, it is Boswell who made him so": without Boswell, the reputation of Johnson--a good and kindly man but neither a great writer nor a great thinker--would be slight.

158. Copeland, Thomas W. "Boswell's Portrait of Burke." The Age of Johnson: Essays Presented to Chauncey Brewster Tinker. Edited by Frederick W. Hilles. New Haven: Yale University Press, 1949. 27-39.

Notes that Boswell's portrait of Burke in the Life is curiously indistinct, "cloudy and unimpressive." Suggests that Burke's style of talk--copious, allusive, rapid--was far more difficult to capture than Johnson's. Traces Boswell's relationship with Burke, a friendship often strained by political differences, Boswell's desire for patronage, and Burke's reluctance to take Boswell's intellectual capacities seriously.

159. Gulick, Sidney L., Jr. "Johnson, Chesterfield, and Boswell." The Age of Johnson: Essays Presented to Chauncey Brewster Tinker. Edited by F.W. Hilles. New Haven: Yale University Press, 1949. 329-40.

Examines gaps and discrepancies in Boswell's account of Johnson's relationship with Lord Chesterfield and the circumstances leading to the writing of the famous letter. Suggests that Johnson's attitude toward Chesterfield mellowed over the years, and that Boswell's version is unfair to Chesterfield, colored by personal antagonism.

160. Lewis, Wilmarth Sheldon. "The Young Waterman." Virginia Quarterly Review 25 (1949): 66-73.

Suggests that the most delightful passages in the Life are not the set-pieces--the dinner with Wilkes, the visit to the King's Library--but the seemingly accidental, haphazard anecdotes, for example, Johnson's rewarding with a double fare the sculler who desired knowledge of the Argonauts.

161. Horne, Colin J. "Boswell, Burke, and the Life of Johnson." Notes and Queries 195 (1950): 498-99.

Calls attention to a notice appearing in the St. James Chronicle and the Morning Chronicle, probably written by Boswell, claiming that six hundred copies of the Life had been sold in the first week, far outselling Burke's Reflections on the Revolution in France.

162. Stevenson, Robert. "`The Rivals'--Hawkins, Burney, and Boswell." Musical Quarterly 36 (Jan. 1950): 67-82.

Claims that Hawkins's character and literary achievement were distorted both by Burney and by Boswell, who envied his intimacy with Johnson and feared him as a biographical competitor.

163. Powell, Lawrence. F. "A Task Ended." Johnson Society Transactions 1949-1950. Lichfield: 1951. 17-25.

Reflects upon the completed revision of Hill's edition of the Life, noting both the additions to the Johnson canon and identification of anonymous persons that can now be made with certainty.

164. Baldwin, Louis. "The Conversation in Boswell's Life of Johnson." Journal of English and Germanic Philology 51 (1952): 492-506.

Considers the authenticity of Johnson's conversation in the Life by examining the reliability of Boswell's memory, his method of preserving Johnson's talk, his special qualifications for the task--admiration for Johnson, love of accuracy--and contemporary opinion on the genuineness of the conversation. Concludes that Boswell does provide a faithful record of Johnson, that he quotes "the real Dr. Johnson practically verbatim."

165. Hart, Edward. "The Contributions of John Nichols to Boswell's Life of Johnson." PMLA 67 (1952): 391-40.

Shows that John Nichols assisted Boswell in preparing the Life by advising him concerning its printing and publication and by supplying him with letters and anecdotes.

166. Taylor, F. "Johnsoniana from the Bagshawe Muniments in the John Rylands Library: Sir James Caldwell, Dr. Hawkesworth, Dr. Johnson, and Boswell's Use of the `Caldwell Minute.'" John Rylands Library Bulletin 35 (Sept. 1952): 211-47. Reprint. Item 216.

Calls attention to manuscripts of literary interest found among the papers of Sir James Caldwell, friend and correspondent of Lady Mary Wortley Montagu, John Hawkesworth, and Johnson, most notably the Caldwell Minute, Johnson's own account of his conversation with George III and Boswell's main source for his version in the Life. Compares the Minute with the manuscript of the Life to reveal Boswell's method: he copied out the text of the former and simply made verbal alterations intended to improve the overall effect.

167. Chapman, R.W. "The Making of the Life of Johnson." Johnsonian and Other Essays and Reviews. London: Oxford University Press, 1953. 20-36.

Reviews volumes 1-6 of Scott's edition of the Private Papers of James Boswell from Malahide Castle and calls attention to what they reveal about Boswell's biographical method: he did not copy Johnson's words verbatim in his presence but rather employed his own system of taking shorthand notes soon after a conversation and later expanding them; the heart of the Life is to be found in Boswell's journals, and Malone's role in the composition and editing of the Life was greater than previously believed.

168. Adams, Sarah F. "Boswell's Life of Samuel Johnson." Yale University Library Gazette 29 (1954): 35-36.

Describes a copy of the first edition of the Life with two uncanceled leaves and calls attention to Boswell's substantial revisions of passages concerning the poet James Grainger and Johnson's opinions on conjugal fidelity.

169. Fifer, Charles N. "Dr. Johnson and Bennet Langton." Journal of English and Germanic Philology 54 (1955): 504-6.

Believes that Boswell's account of Langton's first meeting with Johnson mistakenly implies that Langton introduced himself as a complete stranger. Suggests that Johnson knew or had at least heard of Langton's father, the acquaintance of Spence, Garrick, Robert Dodsley, and Joseph Warton.

170. Kronenberger, Lewis. "Johnson and Boswell." The Republic of Letters: Essays on Various Writers. New York: Alfred A. Knopf, 1955. 89-123.

Considers Boswell and Johnson "inseparable," each owing his fame to the other: Johnson, "the greatest social talker whose talk has ever been recorded," and Boswell, "the greatest biographer the world has ever known." Praises Boswell's biographical gifts--industry, judgment, and an instinct for the dramatic--while conceding that the portrait of Johnson in the Life is perhaps too simple and too static.

171. Sherbo, Arthur. "Gleanings from Boswell's `Notebook.'" Notes and Queries 201 (1956): 108-12.

Reviews details of Johnson's life--his fondness for oatmeal porridge, the details of a quarrel with Dr. Thomas Barnard--recorded by Boswell in private papers but not included in the text of the Life.

172. Edel, Leon. Literary Biography. London: Rupert Hart-Davis, 1957. 13-20. Reprint. "Boswell." Writing Lives: Principia Biographica. New York: Norton, 1984. 42-58.

Notes the advantages enjoyed by Boswell, a biographer who worked from life rather than from documents; he not only observed his subject firsthand, but also created incidents and arranged encounters in the life he planned to write. In a sense, then, "Boswell helped to live the biography he would ultimately write," thus blurring the line between biography and autobiography. Boswell lacked, on the other hand, the objectivity and perspective which can be achieved only by the biographer working at some distance from his subject.

173. Garraty, John. The Nature of Biography. New York: Alfred A. Knopf, 1957. 25-28, 93-99.

Believes that Boswell's Life, though "universally admired," remains a special case, a poor biographical model. Though it embodies a passion for accuracy and completeness characteristic of modern biography, the Life is "one man's recollection of another," and therefore lacks proportion as well as the distance required to evaluate its subject's career and place in history.

174. Todd, William B. "Cowper's Commentary on the Life of Johnson." Times Literary Supplement, 15 Mar. 1957: 168.

Transcribes William Cowper's observations on the Life preserved in Johnny Johnson's annotated edition.

175. Morgan, H.A. "Boswell and Macaulay." Contemporary Review 193 (1958): 27-29.

Characterizes Macaulay's abuse of Boswell's character and intellect as unjustified and malicious.

176. Bernard, F.V. "Two Errors in Boswell's Life of Johnson." Notes and Queries 6 (1959): 280-81.

Challenges Boswell's claim that Johnson rarely used parentheses and never used the phrases "the former" and "the latter."

177. Butt, John. James Boswell. University of Edinburgh Inaugural Lecture No. 3, 11 Dec. 1959. Edinburgh: Oliver and Boyd, Ltd., 1959.

Warns against the dangers of treating Boswell solely as a peculiar personality and thus ignoring his biographical achievement: his ability to remember, record, and recreate imaginatively Johnson's conversation; his gift not only for drawing Johnson out in conversation but also for leading him into memorable situations; his devotion to research, adherence to Johnson's biographical principles, and development of a new narrative method.

178. De Beer, E.S. "Macaulay and Croker: The Review of Croker's Boswell." Review of English Studies, n.s. 10 (1959): 388-97.

Examines the accusation that Macaulay's harsh review of Croker's edition of Boswell's Life was revenge for humiliating defeats suffered in parliamentary debates. Finds that the Croker-Macaulay encounters were not decisive, and that even though Macaulay hated Croker, the edition was in fact badly done, the notes inaccurate, the shape of the Life marred by Croker's interpolations.

179. Lonsdale, Roger. "Dr. Burney and the Integrity of Boswell's Quotations." Papers of the Bibliographical Society of America 53 (1959): 327-31.

Shows that the text of letters from Johnson to Burney printed in the Life was altered not by Boswell but by Burney himself, who sought to conceal Johnson's authorship of the dedications to his History of Music and his Account...of the Commemoration of Handel.

180. Pottle, Frederick A. "The Dark Hints of Sir John Hawkins and Boswell." Modern Language Notes 56 (1941): 325-29. Revised and reprinted in New Light on Dr. Johnson: Essays on the Occasion of his 250th Birthday. Edited by Frederick W. Hilles. New Haven: Yale University Press, 1959. 153-62.

Re-examines Boswell's and Hawkins's hints that sexual irregularities as a young man caused Johnson's remorse on his deathbed. One of Boswell's journal entries suggests that Hawkins read a portion of Johnson's diary, which was later burned, and informed Boswell that it contained evidence that Johnson had indulged "his strong amorous passions." Speculates that Boswell and Hawkins agreed to mention Johnson's lapses but not to mention their source.

181. Hart, Francis R. "Boswell and the Romantics: A Chapter in the History of Biographical Theory." Journal of English Literary History 27 (1960): 44-65.

Examines Boswell's influence on biographical theory between 1791 and 1831, focusing on the ambivalent responses of readers such as Wordsworth, Hazlitt, and Lockhart: while enthusiastic about Boswell's seemingly naive authenticity and dramatic immediacy, they were skeptical as to the value of preserving minute details, conversations, and letters in biographies, aware that biographical truth involves more than simple factual accuracy, and concerned that such practices would make human relations artificial. Believes that Boswell's example led to greater self-consciousness and impressionism among the Romantics, who assumed that a biography was subjective, colored by the writer's personality and relationship to the subject.

182. Hamilton, Harlan W. "Boswell's Suppression of a Paragraph in Rambler 60." Modern Language Notes 76 (1961): 218-20.

Notes that when quoting Rambler 60 in the Life to justify his own biographical method, Boswell suppresses an entire paragraph, an ellipsis not marked in the edition of Hill and Powell. Speculates that Boswell chose not to quote the paragraph--Johnson's criticism of Racan's use of private conversations in his biography of Malherbe--because it might have been applied to his own method in the Life.

183. Morgan, Lee. "Boswell's Portrait of Goldsmith." Studies in Honor of John C. Hodges and Alwin Thaler. Edited by Richard Beale Davis and John Leon Lievsay. Knoxville: University of Tennessee Press, 1961. 67-76.

Argues that Boswell's portrait of Goldsmith in the Life is "valid and reliable": shows that those faults Boswell does record--Goldsmith's conversational ineptitude, for example, or his envy--are likewise documented by contemporaries such as Davies, Thrale, and Hawkins, often much less sympathetically. Boswell balances these faults with an appreciation of Goldsmith's virtues--loyalty, courage, a willingness to forgive--and of his considerable literary abilities.

184. Verosky, Sister M. Victorine. "John Walker's One Clergyman." Notes and Queries 8 (1961): 126-28.

Identifies the clergyman that John Walker mentions in the Life as John Milner, a Roman Catholic priest who attended Walker's classes in public speaking.

185. Fifer, Charles N. "Boswell and the Decorous Bishop." Journal of English and Germanic Philology 61 (1962): 48-56.

Speculates that Bishop Thomas Percy initiated the break between himself and Boswell because he was angry that Boswell included an unflattering portrait of him in the Life, and refused to suppress anecdotes about his friends or allow his contributions to be published anonymously.

186. Liebert, Herman W. "Boswell's Life of Johnson, 1791." American Notes and Queries 1 (1962): 6-7.

Lists variants in cancels, press numbers, incorrect foliation, and typographical errors among six copies of the Life, 1791.

187. Noyes, Charles E. "Samuel Johnson: Student of Hume." University of Mississippi Studies in English 3 (1962): 91-94.

Argues that the Life demonstrates Johnson's familiarity with Hume and his work: the conversations are full of pronouncements on Hume's style, politics, and morals; and Johnson's denial that Wolfe had defeated Montcalm at the Battle for Quebec shows his mastery of Hume's method in the "Essay on Miracles."

188. Gray, James. "Johnson as Boswell's Moral Tutor." Burke Newsletter 4 (1963): 202-10.

Describes Boswell's search for moral guidance and instruction from Charles de Guiffardiere, Hume, Smith, Rousseau, Voltaire, and Johnson--men who seemed to possess the qualities he most admired: decisiveness, understanding, wisdom. Johnson best understood his yearning for guidance and "the hunger of his imagination": though his advice could not preserve Boswell from his self-destructive tendencies, it may have sustained him in the great labor of writing the Life.

189. Greene, Donald J. "Reflections on a Literary Anniversary." Queen's Quarterly 70 (1963): 198-208. Reprint. Item 216.

Argues that Boswell's omissions and distortions in the Life are responsible for the simplified image of Johnson as a lovable, slightly pompous eccentric rather than as a great writer. Describes

Boswell's Life as an edited diary, far less successful in illuminating Johnson's married life, early years in London, religious and political opinions than Hawkins's. Suggests that Boswell's portrayal of Johnson is motivated by unconscious hostility, a need to cut his master down to size, and that generations of readers have eagerly embraced this watered-down version of a complex genius.

190. Lustig, Irma S. "Boswell's Portrait of Himself in The Life of Samuel Johnson." Dissertation, University of Pennsylvania, 1963.

Argues that though Boswell deferred to Johnson's intellect, he expresses independent religious, political, and literary opinions in the Life, a complex blend of tradition and modernity: Boswell valued both Catholic ritual and direct communion between man and God; he endorsed feudal subordination and supported commercial expansion and the American colonists; he shared Johnson's belief in the moral purpose of literature but recognized the value of Swift and Fielding.

191. Molin, Sven Eric. "Boswell's Account of the Johnson-Wilkes Meeting." Studies in English Literature 3 (1963): 307-22.

Analyzes the famous Johnson-Wilkes episode as a unified dramatic whole, representative of Boswell's artistry in the Life. Shows that Boswell borrows the structure of the Comedy of Manners, complete with five acts, prologue, and epilogue, and employs literary techniques, most notably Dickensian characterization and the shaping, paraphrasing, and pointing of conversation to demonstrate concretely Johnson's good humor and to affirm eighteenth-century social values--learning, politeness, and wit.

192. "The Relationship Between Johnson and Boswell." National Retired Teachers Association Journal 14.3 (1963): 9-11.

Suggests that despite differences in age, temperament, and circumstances, Johnson and Boswell, teacher and pupil, shared a common theory of biography, outlined by Johnson in Rambler 60 and practiced by Boswell in the Life.

193. Altick, Richard D. "Johnson and Boswell." Lives and Letters: A History of Literary Biography in England and America. New York: Alfred A. Knopf, Inc., 1965. 46-74. Reprint. Item 216.

Assesses Boswell's contributions to the developing art of literary biography: the combination of a variety of points of view to create a three-dimensional portrait, a refusal to suppress his subject's weaknesses, the dramatic rendering of scenes and conversations, the inclusion of concrete and specific detail. Notes the weaknesses of the Life--the whole is disorderly, unbalanced, and limited by its scenic, chronological structure--and argues that the influence of the Life, the model of a literary life in the nineteenth century, was not good: in the hands of less skillful imitators, Boswell's method led to the writing of scores of "trivial, irrelevant, and dull" lives.

194. Jack, Ian. "Two Biographers: Lockhart and Boswell." Johnson, Boswell and Their Circle; Essays Presented to Lawrence Fitzroy Powell in Honour of His Eighty-Fourth Birthday. Oxford: Clarendon Press, 1965. 268-85.

Notes similarities in the lives of Boswell and Lockhart--each was a Scottish Tory who studied at Glasgow, became a member of the Faculty of Advocates at Edinburgh, enjoyed literary fame in his twenties, and struggled through personal difficulties to complete a biography of an older, fatherly man. Contrasts their characters--Boswell was boyish, sociable, good humored; Lockhart, aloof, reserved, and cold--and their biographical methods: Boswell energetically collected materials for the Life and enjoyed greater freedom in the use of his sources, while Lockhart took less initiative in gathering material and was forced to revise to accommodate Sir Walter Scott's friends and associates; Boswell lovingly recorded and recreated Johnson's conversation, while Lockhart, though he admired the Life, was less interested in his subject's talk and disapproved of the practice of preserving it; in short, "every detail about Johnson mattered to Boswell, whereas not every detail about Scott mattered to Lockhart."

195. Kendall, Paul Murray. The Art of Biography. New York: Norton, 1965. 98-99, passim.

Argues that Boswell's Life, "the world's greatest biography," embodies the values and traditions of its own age--sociability and common sense--and, in its treatment of eccentricity and madness, its celebration of the individual, anticipates the world of the French Revolution.

196. Lustig, Irma S. "Boswell on Politics in The Life of Johnson." PMLA 80 (1965): 387-93.

Describes Boswell as "an amalgam of traditionalist and rebel": he adhered to old-fashioned notions of feudal subordination, and, at the same time, embraced certain modern principles of reform. By proclaiming himself a Tory, Boswell announced his loyalty to King and Church, although he opposed the government of George III on its handling of Wilkes and the American War. Makes a distinction between Boswell's rebellious views of the 1760s and 1770s--his sympathy for the Corsicans and legal defense of those he considered oppressed--and his more conservative views of the 1780s and 1790s, expressed in editorial additions to the Life.

197. Pettit, Henry. "Boswell and Young's Night Thoughts." Notes and Queries, n.s. 12 (1965): 21.

Corrects an annotation in the Hill-Powell edition of the Life: Boswell alludes to an affecting passage in Young's Night Thoughts describing the gradual death of Lucia rather than of Narcissa.

198. Butt, John. "James Boswell." Biography in the Hands of Walton, Johnson, and Boswell. Ewing Lectures. Los Angeles: University of California Press, 1966. 33-48.

Revises Item 177 to show that Boswell, even as a young man, shared important biographical opinions with Johnson and to note that Boswell "shares Johnson's and Walton's care for the particular, in the illusion of character."

199. Camp, Truman W. "Boswell and Johnson's Principles of Biography." CEA Critic, Apr. 1966: 11, 14.

Asserts that in the Life, Boswell puts into practice Johnson's own biographical theories; just as Rambler 60 advises, Boswell writes an instructive and intimate account, full of circumstantial detail, while refusing to idealize his subject.

200. Lustig, Irma S. "Boswell's Literary Criticism in The Life of Johnson." Studies in English Literature 6 (1966): 529-41.

Believes that Boswell's literary opinions, consistently neglected and undervalued, reveal "his competence and modernity" as a critic. Though Boswell shared with Johnson a belief in the moral purpose of literature, he was a more enthusiastic reader of the sentimental and pathetic literature popular in the late eighteenth century--Young, Ossian, Gray. Shows that Boswell was a perceptive critic both of comtemporary literature--unlike Johnson, he admired Swift and Fielding--and of Johnson's works--his judgments in the Life on the strengths and limitations of Johnson's prose, for example, are discriminating and sophisticated.

201. Reed, Joseph W., Jr. "Boswell and After." English Biography in the Early Nineteenth Century 1801-1838. Yale Studies in English 160. New Haven: Yale University Press, 1966. 3-26.

Characterizes the attitude of nineteenth-century critics toward Boswell as condescending: he is readable and amusing, an indefatigable collector, but not an artist. Although there were isolated attempts to preserve conversation and anecdotes remained popular, there were no full-scale biographies that imitated Boswell's method written in the nineteenth century.

202. De Beer, E.S. "Dr. Powell's Index to Boswell's Life of Johnson." Indexer 5 (1967): 135-39.

Describes Powell's method of compiling an index to his edition of the Life and praises it as "a most efficient and most appropriate complement to the text."

203. Palmer, Joyce Arline Cornette. "Boswell's Life of Johnson as Literary History." Dissertation, University of Tennessee, 1967.

Argues that Boswell employed many of the techniques of literary history--information on sources, revision, influence, literary developments and controversies--though the Life is not a genuine literary history in the tradition of Thomas Warton's.

204. Powell, Lawrence F. "A Boswellian Identification." Times Literary Supplement, 30 Mar. 1967: 274.

Identifies Richard How, a correspondent of Boswell, misnamed by Malone in a note to the third edition of the Life.

205. Rewa, Michael. "Boswell's Life of Johnson, IV, 420-421." Notes and Queries, n.s. 14 (1967): 411-12.

Finds that William Gerard Hamilton's remark on Johnson's death ("He has made a chasm...") echoes an observation in Rambler 6.

206. Greene, Donald J. "The Uses of Autobiography in the Eighteenth Century." Essays in Eighteenth-Century Biography. Edited by Philip B. Daghlian. Bloomington: Indiana University Press, 1968. 43-66.

Calls for greater attention to be paid eighteenth-century autobiography by asserting the superiority of Johnson's autobiographical fragment to Boswell's Life, claiming that it presents "authentic reports of subjective states" rather than a biographer's conjecture, that it contains "a far greater concentration" of psychologically significant detail, and that the autobiographer's own tone reveals the subject directly rather than through the distortions of the biographer's preoccupations and biases.

207. Passler, David Luther. "Time, Form and Style in Boswell's Life of Johnson." Dissertation, University of North Carolina at Chapel Hill, 1968.

See Item 223.

208. Rader, Ralph W. "Literary Form in Factual Narrative: The Example of Boswell's Johnson." Essays in Eighteenth-Century Biography. Edited by Philip B. Daghlian. Bloomington: Indiana University Press, 1968. 3-42. Reprint. Item 278.

Believes that only a handful of factual narratives rank as literature, those works--Boswell's Life, Gibbon's Decline and Fall, for example--that "transcend while fulfilling the usual purpose of history and biography, to provide true knowledge of the human past" and "raise their subjects out of the past and represent them to the imagination as concrete, self-intelligible causes of emotion." Argues that those who criticize the structure of the Life fail to understand that the book's real subject is not Johnson's life but his character, Boswell's purpose to make readers feel for themselves the reverence and admiration Johnson inspired. Identifies this image of Johnson as the source of the Life's unity: every part--each aphorism, each anecdote, each scene--gives pleasure in itself and also concretely manifests the image of Johnson as a great and good man. Concludes that although "certified truth" is a requisite for all factual narratives, the great truth that Boswell captures is the essential truth of Johnson's character, his essence, which the discovery of new facts will not alter, and which is universal in its appeal: "self-validating, self-intelligible, inherently moving, permanently valuable."

209. Alkon, Paul K. "Boswell's Control of Aesthetic Distance." University of Toronto Quarterly 38 (1969): 174-91. Reprint. Item 216.

Argues that Boswell's success as a biographer lies in large part in his ability to manipulate the distance between his subject and his readers through a variety of devices. By blurring the distinction between past and present and between thought and word, and by intruding with his own beliefs into the Life, Boswell creates intellectual dramas in which readers are invited to participate: they must enter the debate themselves, agree with Johnson or Boswell or another of the participants. Boswell also controls aesthetic distance by playing roles: as a literate Everyman, he collapses the distance between reader and narrator--"He becomes one of us"; as a member of the Johnson circle, he calls attention to "his own distinctiveness," reminding readers of his special status. In the role of Johnsonian sage, Boswell again moves away from readers toward Johnson, generalizing on the human condition and offering advice. Concludes that Boswell loses control of aesthetic distance occasionally--our laughter at the narrator deflects attention from his subject--but these lapses are comparatively few--"the weakness is not fatal."

210. Amory, Hugh. "Boswell in Search of the Intentional Fallacy." Bulletin of the New York Public Library 73 (1969): 25-39.

Describes the Life as a kind of mock Socratic dialogue: Johnson the unkempt sage, Boswell the pupil and searcher after truth, the Life itself dialectically structured. Warns that Boswell's changing intentions and his conscious shaping of material cannot be ignored.

211. Clements, Richard. "Erskine for the Defense." New Rambler: Journal of the Johnson Society of London, Jan. 1969: 2-16.

Contains a biographical account of Thomas Erskine (1750-1823), a brilliant lawyer and Lord Chancellor of England, whose meeting and conversation with Johnson in 1772 Boswell records in the Life.

212. Hankins, John R. "The Eighteenth-Century English Biographer and His Sources." Dissertation, Case Western Reserve University, 1969.

Discusses the increased use of letters and personal writings by eighteenth-century biographers, challenging the belief that Mason and Boswell were the first to include letters in biographies. Examines Boswell's use of personal documents and his influence on later eighteenth-century lives.

213. Gwiasda, Karl Eric. "The Boswell Biographers: A Study of Life and Letters Writing in the Victorian Period." Dissertation, Northwestern University, 1969.

Traces the influence of Boswell's biographical method on Carlyle's Sterling, Gaskell's Charlotte Bronte, Forster's Landor and Dickens, Trevelyan's Macaulay, and Froude's Carlyle.

214. Waingrow, Marshall. Introduction. The Correspondence and Other Papers of James Boswell Relating to the Making of the Life of Johnson. The Yale Editions of the Private Papers of James Boswell, Research Edition. Correspondence, Vol. 2. Edited by Marshall Waingrow. New York: McGraw-Hill, 1969. xxi-l. Reprint. Item 216.

Provides a documentary history of the Life, explaining that in addition to Boswell's journal and the manuscript, more than four hundred letters and other papers--evidence of Boswell's extensive research--went into its making. Believes that a close examination of Boswell's editorial practices, of his revisions and omissions, demonstrates that the finished Life is both an authentic and a unified portrait, a book remarkable not only for its fullness but also for its wholeness: when Boswell paraphrases or expands his sources, most often he does so to accommodate these various materials in clashing styles to a finished, polished narrative. That he is no mere compiler is likewise clear from his revisions in content: he occasionally rewrites sources to eliminate what he perceives of as distortions. Answers objections that Boswell suppresses references to Johnson's failings--his excessive drinking and eating, use of drugs, sexual irregularities--by pointing out that each is admitted to the work in some form and arguing that other information is omitted because it contradicts Boswell's own experience, his interpretation of Johnson as a man whose mind, his greatest strength, triumphs over its own tendency to prey upon itself.

215. Benjamin, Curtis G. "An Author's Progress." Scholarly Publishing 2 (1970): 25-31.

Prints a "Chronology of the Making of the Life," excerpted from Item 214.

216. Clifford, James L., ed. Twentieth-Century Interpretations of Boswell's Life of Johnson. Englewood Cliffs, NJ: Prentice Hall, 1970.

Contains Items 6, 82, 105, 109, 115, 135, 166, 189, 193, 209, 214, 217, 219.

217. Clifford, James L. Introduction. Twentieth-Century Interpretations of Boswell's Life of Johnson. Englewood Cliffs, NJ: Prentice Hall, 1970. 1-26.

Notes that only since the discovery of his archives in the 1920s has Boswell been afforded the attention of a great artist. Since then, however, scholars and critics--the most important of whom are represented in this volume--have examined Boswell's method of keeping a journal; his private system of daily memoranda, shorthand notes, and expanded entries; the accuracy of his reporting--a comparison of Boswell's journal and the diary of his contemporary Dr. Thomas Campbell confirms his essential reliability--and his method of composing the Life, from gathering--and skeptically evaluating--secondhand anecdotes through his painstaking rewriting of the manuscript for color and precision. Notes finally that many contemporary readers of Boswell's Hebrides and the Life were offended by their candor; in the nineteenth century, Boswell's works were considered valuable repositories of information; only in the twentieth century have they been treated as great works of art.

218. Hart, Paxton. "The Presentation of Oliver Goldsmith in Boswell's Life of Johnson." re: arts and letters 3.2 (1970): 4-15.

Disagrees with those nineteenth-century biographers of Goldsmith who find Boswell's portrayal of him hostile and inaccurate, arguing instead that Boswell offers "a remarkably balanced portrayal," revealing both his envy, ignorance, and folly, as well as his sympathy, humor, and genius. Explains that Boswell's presentation of Goldsmith is necessarily incomplete in the Life, where Goldsmith is important mainly as a foil for Johnson.

219. Pottle, Frederick A. "The Life of Johnson: Art and Authenticity." Twentieth-Century Interpretations of Boswell's Life of Johnson. Edited by James L. Clifford. Englewood Cliffs, NJ: Prentice-Hall, 1970. 66-73.

Notes that Boswell in describing his achievement in the Life stressed its authenticity and his own diligence as a collector rather than its art and his own literary skill. Argues that it is erroneous to view the Life solely as the product of a good memory and hard work. Describes Boswell's method of composition: first, he wrote notes, often disorderly and hurried, that served to aid his memory; next, he expanded these notes into full entries; finally, in transferring material from the journal to the Life, he expanded entries again, often adding new details, gathering "a second crop of memory," sometimes expanding the original rough notes for the first time. Calls Johnson's conversation as reported by Boswell in the Life "an imaginative reconstruction": they are authentic--Boswell invents nothing--and artistic--he does condense and shape Johnson's utterances, based on his own intuitive understanding of Johnson's style.

220. Greene, Donald J. "The Making of Boswell's Life of Johnson." Studies in Burke and His Time 12 (1970-71): 1812-20.

Reviews Item 214, calling it "far and away the most valuable volume in the collection so far" for students of Johnson, and claiming that the new information it contains completely undermines the Life as an independent source: "No responsible scholar is going to rest content with Boswell's final doctored version of Johnson when the undoctored materials are available."

221. Lambert, Joseph Patrick. "Boswell as a Critic of Johnson's Literature." Dissertation, Auburn University, 1971.

Praises Boswell's ability as a critic and describes his blending of biography and criticism in the Life as a refinement of Johnson's method.

222. Lonsdale, Roger. "Two Boswell Identifications." Notes and Queries, n.s. 18 (1971): 337.

Corrects two vague identifications--of Richard Pottinger and John Warltire--in Waingrow's Correspondence and Other Papers Relating to the Making of the Life.

223. Passler, David Luther. Time, Form and Style in Boswell's Life of Johnson. New Haven: Yale University Press, 1971.

Examines the narrative techniques Boswell employs in the Life to enhance dramatic immediacy and to imbue his essentially static portrait of Johnson with the "feeling of lively motion." Boswell mixes time levels in his narrative, moving rapidly from the historical moment up to the time of composition; he combines conventions of the fixed ana tradition and the progressive journal form; he assumes a variety of narrative stances (frustrated biographer, moralizer); he varies the narrative pace and his prose style, and in so doing, creates a complex composite portrait of his subject, "a celebration of Johnson's changelessness": he "holds Johnson up for our view and slowly rotates him, like a huge cut gem, to display his many facets."

224. Steese, Peter. "Boswell `Walking upon Ashes.'" English Symposium Papers, Vol. I. Edited by Douglas Shepherd. Fredonia, NY: State University of New York College at Fredonia, 1971. 46-69.

Examines Boswell's revision of a passage from the journal into the Life--the initial meeting with Johnson on 16 May 1763--to demonstrate that "Boswell is not taking untoward liberties in order to create an exciting scene": Boswell changes few essential facts; his alterations in Johnson's conversation are the product of his enhanced ability to recreate Johnson's language; and Boswell's additional "personal reactions" and careful structuring of the scene reflect an understanding of events achieved only with distance, not a distortion. Concludes that Boswell's practice is evidence that factual narratives may be both "dramatic" and also "true to life."

225. Baxter, Mary Ruth Sandvold. "James Boswell: The Imagination of a Biographer." Dissertation, Ohio State University, 1972.

Explores how Boswell developed the image of Johnson which informs the Life and what literary techniques he employed in order to subordinate Johnson's shortcomings to his heroic virtues.

226. Lustig, Irma S. "Boswell at Work: The 'Animadversions' on Mrs. Piozzi." Modern Language Review 67 (1972): 11-30.

Analyzes Boswell's revision of passages in the Life attacking Piozzi and her Anecdotes. Shows that Boswell, with the assistance of John Courtenay, painstakingly rewrote and reshaped his remarks in order to discredit her account of Johnson and reveal her ingratitude while eliminating evidence of personal antagonism.

227. Renner, Michael Friel. "The Literary Art of James Boswell." Dissertation, Claremont Graduate School, 1972.

Explores the relationship between Boswell and Johnson, notes both the combative and warm aspects of their friendship, and characterizes the Life as an expression of that friendship.

228. Tracy, Clarence. "Boswell: The Cautious Empiricist." The Triumph of Culture: 18th-Century Perspectives. Edited by Paul Fritz and David Williams. Toronto: A.M. Hakkert, 1972. 225-43.

Argues that from Johnson, Boswell learned the necessity of grounding biography on "masses of verifiable fact" while maintaining an intense skepticism about the value and truth of anecdotal sources. Boswell's method is to combine his observations with secondhand accounts--just the sort of material Johnson distrusted--while declining to interpret his facts or draw conclusions from them. The Life, therefore, is shapeless, weakened by superficial treatment of important topics--Johnson's relationship with his wife and Thrale, his writings. Concludes that Boswell's Johnson, though shaped and limited by facts and thus not an invention, is an imaginative creation, a product of Boswell's preoccupations and psychic needs; Boswell's facts serve a rhetorical function: they inspire confidence in his readers about his reliability as a biographer.

229. Woolley, James D. "Johnson as Despot: Anna Seward's Rejected Contribution to Boswell's Life." Modern Philology 70 (1972): 140-45.

Speculates that Boswell chose not to include Anna Seward's account of Johnson's conversation with the Quaker Mary Knowles on 15 April 1778 for rhetorical reasons: to include this hostile dramatization of Johnson's intolerance would have been to damage his own portrayal of Johnson as an admirable character.

230. Alkon, Paul K. "Boswellian Time." Studies in Burke and His Time 14 (1973): 239-56.

Argues that Boswell believed that authenticity depended on the relationship between reading time and read-about time: "Only insofar as the reader's experience of a biography approaches the duration of the subject's existence will there be any likelihood of accurate mimesis"--hence the great bulk of the life. Boswell's adaptation of the unity of time achieves this ideal--correspondence between experience and representation--in a limited sense by confining himself to recording only significant actions. Boswell's notion of authenticity required also that readers experience a life for themselves: he shifted from conceiving the Life as static--a painting, a mausoleum--to thinking of it as kinetic--a succession of scenes to be lived through. Readers of the Life have a sense of being in Johnson's company in part because it requires a long time to read the book but also because Boswell prolongs the sense of duration through a variety of means: he devotes more and more pages to less and less real time lived by Johnson and thus slows the tempo; he calls attention to dates and so compels a reader to notice the flow of time; he inserts letters, the reading of which collapses the distinction between real and recorded time; he jumbles together different time levels and avoids devices--suspense, transitions--that might quicken the pace. Shows that Boswell likewise observed a kind of unity of place: Johnson is almost always in London, talking, thus further blurring the boundaries between eposides and therefore expanding the Life's duration.

231. Damrosch, Leopold, Jr. "The Life of Johnson: An Anti-Theory." Eighteenth-Century Studies 6 (1973): 486-505.

Claims that the Life, despite its many excellences--the dramatic scenes, the moving descriptive passages--is not "a fully realized work of art." Believes the Life is marred, first of all, by structural and organizational defects: too much emphasis is placed on Johnson as an older, sometimes irritable and abusive man; not enough attention is paid to Johnson's literary achievement or the true nature of his melancholy. Argues further that Boswell's presence as narrator likewise weakens the Life: he is "an intrusive and annoying figure," intellectually feeble, whose tone is often pompous, pretentious, and snobbish.

232. Hubbard, Murray Phillip. "Boswell in the Nineteenth-Century: A Study of his Reputation in Britain, 1795-1900." Dissertation, Kansas State University, 1973.

Challenges the view that Macaulay's criticism of Boswell was representative of nineteenth-century critical opinion: shows that Boswell was praised by nineteenth-century critics for many of the same qualities that modern critics have pointed to: his literary skill and imaginative power.

233. Sheehan, Joseph. "The `Voice' of Boswell in His Life of Samuel Johnson." Dissertation, Catholic University of America, 1973.

Offers a rhetorical analysis of the Life and describes Boswell's voice in it as gentlemanly, moral, moderate, and sensible.

234. Nussbaum, Felicity A. "Boswell's Treatment of Johnson's Temper: `A Warm West-Indian Climate.'" Studies in English Literature 14 (1974): 421-33.

Argues that Boswell's handling of Johnson's temper is authentic--he shows Johnson's anger truly, refusing to suppress a real flaw--and artistic--he shapes his material carefully, balancing Johnson's temper and his benevolence. Examines passages in the journals and in the manuscript version of the Life that describe Johnson's outbursts and analyzes Boswell's revisions: in order to portray Johnson as a great and good man despite occasional displays of irritation, Boswell softens his language, places angry remarks in the larger context of a sincere friendship, reasserts Johnson's dignity, emphasizes his willingness to reconcile after harsh words, and rearranges conversation so that Johnson's more agreeable traits dominate.

235. Pottle, Frederick A. "The Adequacy as Biography of Boswell's Life of Johnson." Transactions of the Johnson Society. Lichfield: 1974. 6-19. Reprint. Item 278.

Responds to charges made by Greene and Damrosch that Boswell's Life is inaccurate and structurally flawed. Argues that what Greene wants is not a literary life--an imaginatively shaped narrative--but a chronology--a factual record of specific events in an author's life with no value judgments. Believes that Rader has adequately answered questions about the Life's uneven proportions by showing that "the organizing principle of the book is a massive idea or image of Johnson's character." Disagrees also with the claim of Greene and Damrosch that Boswell fails to do justice to Johnson as a writer: Boswell does call attention to Johnson's writings and makes some critical remarks but wisely concentrates on the human personality--the domain of biography--rather than the literary personality--the domain of criticism--and does not engage in extended literary criticism, which is certain to become dated. Agrees, finally, with Damrosch that Boswell does make annoying intrusions in the Life, that the public Boswell is often pompous, unlike the Boswell of the journals, whose style is "tentative, self-doubting, and unpretentious," whose opinions are "generally interesting, often charming, often acute."

236. Wimsatt, William K., Jr. "Images of Samuel Johnson." Journal of English Literary History 41 (1974): 359-74.

Reaffirms Boswell's imaginative genius by contrasting his portrayal of Johnson with those of other contemporary biographers--Hawkins, Thrale, and Fanny Burney--all of whom produce images inferior to Boswell's: Hawkins writes in a pedestrian style, cannot understand Johnson's generosity or compassion, and includes very little of his conversation; Thrale's portrait of Johnson, marred by inaccuracies, repetition, and an inadequate narrative sense, depicts Johnson as a grotesque savage; and Fanny Burney, though a better dramatist than Thrale and an imaginative artist in her own right, "gives us characteristically a picture of an excited little girl being cuddled by an affectionate, if frightful-looking old bear."

237. Nicholls, Graham. " 'The Race with Death': Samuel Johnson and a Sense of Ending." Transactions of the Johnson Society. Lichfield: 1975. 17-28.

In a discussion of Johnson's attitudes towards conclusions, departures, and death, notes how prominently partings figure in the Life, from Boswell and Johnson's poignant leave-taking at Harwich to their final parting in London twenty years later.

238. Basney, Lionel. "`Ah ha!--Sam Johnson!--I See Thee': Johnson's Ironic Roles." South Atlantic Quarterly 75 (1976): 198-211.

Suggests that Boswell, who valued Johnson's constancy of character as a balance to his own instability, often failed to understand Johnson's ironic self-commentary, role-playing, and mimicry--means by which Johnson developed a sympathetic understanding of other perspectives.

239. Schwalm, David E. "The Life of Johnson: Boswell's Rhetoric and Reputation." Texas Studies in Literature and Language: A Journal of the Humanities 18 (1976): 240-89.

Attempts to resolve the paradox of Boswell's reputation--the Life is considered a great book, but Boswell is not considered a great writer--through a rhetorical analysis of the Life. Argues that Boswell enhances his credibility by concealing his artistry: the narrator appears as an editor or compiler who relies not so much on his own judgment as on the objective material and expert opinion he has so diligently gathered. Suggests that Boswell's commitment to a full and faithful portrait of Johnson leads him to include material from the journal which, when transferred to the Life, makes him appear in an unflattering light. Believes that this necessity becomes a virtue: the figure of Boswell, with all his human weakness, provides readers with a normative standard by which Johnson's greatness may be measured and a point of view from which they may experience Johnson vicariously.

240. Wilson, Paul Carrol. "The Literal Imagination: Johnson and Eighteenth-Century Literature." Dissertation, University of Virginia, 1976.

Views Boswell's Life as the product of the eighteenth century's demand for literal, objectively verified truth: Boswell emphasizes facts and minimizes or conceals his interpretations.

241. Mudrick, Marvin. "The Entertainer." Hudson Review 30 (1977): 270-78.

Reviews Item 214, noting Boswell's reputation for being ungentlemanly and merely entertaining, and showing that several passages revealing the mutual love of Boswell and Johnson--neither gentlemanly nor entertaining--were omitted from the Life.

242. Siebenschuh, William R. "The Relationship Between Factual Accuracy and Literary Art in the Life of Johnson." Modern Philology 74 (1977): 273-88.

Notes that while in the past Boswell was praised as an accurate recorder and a tireless collector of facts, now he is recognized as a sophisticated artist, capable of shaping, suppressing, and rewriting his sources in order to make them conform to his controlling image of Johnson, the source of the Life's unity. Believes that Boswell's factual data creates an illusion, analogous to verisimilitude in fiction, an impression that Johnson is revealed warts and all, when actually Boswell is interpreting, selecting, shaping: "His artistry proceeds virtually undetectable, and is doubly effective in large part because it masquerades successfully as total candor and slavish adherence to the facts." Argues that Boswell, with two exceptions, never "seriously exceeds the proper bounds of the pointedly interpretative or speculative biographer": although he creates the impression of greater factual accuracy than the Life actually possesses and manipulates his sources in ways modern scholars find unacceptable, he does so in order to convey more important, more general, interpretative "truths" about Johnson.

243. Bradham, Jo Allen. "Boswell's Narrative of Oliver Edwards." Journal of Narrative Technique 8 (1978): 176-84.

Examines how Boswell transforms unpromising material--Johnson's encounter with Edwards, his fellow collegian at Oxford--into a fascinating narrative. By constructing a narrative frame, employing theatrical conventions, and controlling patterns of imagery, Boswell contrasts the two men: Edwards, though he claimed that cheerfulness was always breaking in upon his attempts at philosophy, is morbid and gloomy, associated with death and decay; Johnson, on the other hand, the true philosopher, cheerfully affirms life.

244. Dowling, William C. "Boswell and the Problem of Biography." Studies in Biography. Harvard English Studies 8. Edited by Daniel Aaron. Cambridge: Harvard University Press, 1978. 73-93.

Notes that critics have been reluctant to recognize factual works such as Boswell's Life as autonomous, as "self-contained worlds of motive." Claims that the distinction between factual and imaginative literature, between history and art, is false: the terms simply represent different perspectives from which a work may be viewed. Believes genuine literary criticism of the Life begins, therefore, by treating Boswell's Johnson solely as a literary character, like Shakespeare's Macbeth, without any reference to the real Johnson: Johnson is the hero of the Life, Boswell the narrator, London the setting, Garrick and Reynolds minor characters. Analyzes the "symbolic dimensions of the narrator-hero relationship" as an example of such criticism: Boswell, in the tradition of Walton and Roper, presents himself as a naive narrator, a representative of the ordinary, to present Paoli and Johnson as heroes in an unheroic age.

245. Greene, Donald J. " 'Tis a Pretty Book, Mr. Boswell, But--'." Georgia Review 32 (1978): 17-43.

Evaluates Boswell's Life according to modern standards of accuracy, completeness, discrimination, and sympathy, and finds "grave faults indeed": Boswell ignored much of Johnson's writing, misunderstood his political views, failed to evaluate sources critically, left large gaps in the record of Johnson's life, displayed unconscious hostility toward Johnson, organized the book mechanically, and wrote badly. Claims that the Life is not a biography at all but rather a memoir or table talk. Suggests that the book be broken up into its component parts, the conversations extracted and published separately, thus encouraging students of Johnson to examine modern biographies and modern editions of the letters and Prayers and Meditations. Responds to defenders of Boswell's artistry by maintaining that the distinction between imaginative literature and biography must not be blurred; questions of truth cannot be overlooked in biographical writing. Concludes that Boswell's Johnson--"the quaint old `personality'"--should be rejected along with Macaulay's Boswell, for the same reason: the portrait, however memorable and artistic readers have found it, is simply inaccurate.

246. Schwartz, Richard B. Boswell's Johnson: A Preface to the Life. Madison: University of Wisconsin Press, 1978.

Argues that the Life, rather than being a great biography, is instead "essentially a book about Boswell, a portion of his autobiography." Claims that Boswell's biographical method is quasi-scientific: he collects but does not shape data; he does not possess a satisfactory controlling image of Johnson. Suggests also that Boswell fails to understand and accurately portray Johnson's views on topics such as religion and politics; he distorts and misinterprets Johnson in order to make him reflect his own prejudices and enthusiasms. Concludes that students of Johnson may find a full, complex, and accurate portrayal of Johnson--what's missing in the Life--among his own writings.

247. Greene, Donald J. "Do We Need a Biography of Johnson's 'Boswell' Years?" Modern Language Studies 9.3 (1979): 128-36.

Argues that Clifford's Young Sam Johnson and Dictionary Johnson should be supplemented by a third volume and that a modern scholarly biographer will be more accurate, more balanced, and more objective than Boswell. Includes a graph and tables showing the number of days Boswell met with Johnson and the number of pages in the Life devoted to each year from 1763 to 1784.

248. Kirkley, Harriet. "Boswell's Life of the Poet." Journal of Narrative Technique 9 (1979): 21-32.

Praises Boswell's handling of Johnson's early years--from childhood through the publication of the Rambler--and suggests that Boswell models this portion of the Life on Johnson's Lives of the Poets. Notes that Boswell portrays Johnson as a professional writer struggling for independence, borrows Johnsonian rhetorical devices and narrative strategies, shares Johnson's assumption that "the boy is the man in miniature," echoes a number of passages in the Lives, and draws heavily on them for what they reveal about the younger Johnson.

249. Siebenschuh, William R. "Modern Undergraduates and the Accessibility of the Life of Johnson." Eighteenth-Century Life 5.3 (1979): 54-59.

Summarizes the advantages and disadvantages of teaching the Life in an undergraduate course in eighteenth-century British literature: on one hand, it provides a vivid introduction to the age and is itself a brilliant literary achievement, while, on the other hand, it is expensive, long, and requires more background knowledge than most undergraduates bring to it. Recommends that if it is taught, the Life should be read in its entirety, preferably late in the course, after students have read some of Johnson's writings. Suggests that the best approach to the Life is via Boswell's London Journal: Boswell's preoccupations--difficulties with his father, uncertainty about his future, a shifting sense of self--are familiar to undergraduates, and the book introduces an immediately accessible "human drama"--the growing friendship of Boswell and Johnson. By comparing parallel passages in the London Journal and the Life students can explore for themselves Boswell's creative process and the nature of biographical art.

250. Bradham, Jo Allen. "Comic Fragments in the Life of Johnson." Biography 3 (1980): 95-104.

Locates within the seriousness of the Life "comic interludes" that not only invoke laughter but also reveal Johnson's humanity. Analyzes Boswell's use of rhetorical devices--magnification and diminution, anti-climax, irony, animal imagery--to achieve a broad range of comic effects, from farce to mock-heroic.

251. Dowling, William C. "Biographer, Hero, and Audience in Boswell's Life of Johnson." Studies in English Literature 20 (1980): 475-91. Expanded and reprinted as Chapter 5 of Item 638.

Locates two worlds in the Life, both formed around Johnson, the stable moral center: members of an inner sphere--Boswell, Burke, Reynolds, Goldsmith, Langton--venerate Johnson and share his affirmation of traditional wisdom, morality, and belief; those in the outer sphere--freethinkers and philosophes--assault with irony and mockery Johnson's faith and threaten to replace it with infidelity, insincerity, spiritual paralysis. The imaginary readers Boswell addresses, members of his dramatic audience, are invited into and gradually drawn toward the inner circle, where they are allowed to experience Johnson fully, not just as a moralist but also as an eccentric and imperfect man, and to participate in the intellectual drama.

252. Lustig, Irma S. "Fact into Art: James Boswell's Notes, Journals, and the Life of Johnson." Biography in the 18th Century. Edited by John D. Browning. New York: Garland, 1980. 128-46.

Describes the enormous factual record of the Boswell papers at Yale, remarks on Boswell's passion for knowledge of human nature, and reviews his method of composing the Life: the process by which he expanded notes into journal entries and journal entries into the finished Life, his gathering of material from Johnson's acquaintances, and his insertion of "papers apart" within the manuscript of the Life. Analyzes Boswell's two accounts of his first meeting with Johnson to illuminate the art of the journal and the art of the Life and to show how Boswell employs facts as well as literary techniques such as allusion and metaphor to achieve his primary goal, "to re-animate Johnson": Boswell's imaginative reconstruction exhibits "the truth of feeling."

253. Mudrick, Marvin. "Boswell's Johnson." Hudson Review 3 (1980): 279-87.

Reviews J.P. Hardy's Samuel Johnson: A Critical Study, claiming that Johnson's greatness lies not in the "lugubrious commonplaces" of the Rambler but in his "vigorous and incandescent" grasp of particulars, best preserved in Boswell's record of his conversation. Believes Johnson and Boswell "were made for each other": both melancholy, compulsively social, afraid of solitude and death, devoted to rational discourse.

254. Reichard, Hugo M. "Boswell's Johnson, the Hero Made by a Committee." PMLA 95 (1980): 225-33.

Views Boswell's Johnson as an essentially passive hero, a reactor, a man whose life is shaped by the promptings of his associates: they stimulate his conversations, writings, charity, and travel; "they help to shape what he observes, whom he sees, what he thinks about." Argues that Boswell artfully conceals Johnson's dependence, allowing it to function as a subtle counterpoint to the independence and combativeness he emphasizes, making the resulting portrait "a character of rich, contrastive complexity."

255. Dowling, William C. Language and Logos in Boswell's Life of Johnson. Princeton: Princeton University Press, 1981.

Attempts to reconcile objective literary theory with the deconstructive criticism of Derrida through an analysis of narrative discontinuities in the Life: Boswell's narration is only one of many competing worlds of discourse with "a structure of antithetical relations"; at the center of the Life seems to lie the world of Johnson's Prayers and Meditations, "a private world of terror and spiritual anguish," which ultimately fails, as do the other more public worlds, to disclose an actual "Johnsonian presence behind the text of the Life," which itself "enacts a drama of presence and absence." Concludes by calling for a new humanism, based on the shared belief of formalist and deconstructive critics "that language, in its otherness and strangeness, its mysterious opacity, is the true object of humanistic study."

256. Radner, Sanford. "An Unconscious Contract." CEA Critic 43.4 (1981): 13-14.

Believes that Boswell made "an unconscious agreement" with Johnson: in exchange for Johnson's approval, Boswell abandoned a professional literary career. After Johnson's death, Boswell's conflict between his allegiance to his "contract" and his literary ambition was resolved by writing a book that immortalized Johnson.

257. Siebenschuh, William R. "Who Is Boswell's Johnson?" Studies in Eighteenth-Century Culture 10 (1981): 347-60.

Defends Boswell from charges that the Life is an inadequate factual record and that its portrayal of Johnson is seriously distorted. Concedes that Boswell was ignorant of important aspects of Johnson's life and character, but asserts that Boswell's achievement is not his collection of facts but his imaginative vision of Johnson, a vision that is corroborated by Hawkins, Piozzi, and other contemporaries--Boswell's Johnson is their Johnson as well. Suggests that Boswell's use of fictional techniques does not necessarily damage the authenticity of his biography: the dramatizations, for example, are complex interpretative statements that demand the same sort of close analysis that readers traditionally give works of fiction.

258. Barnes, Daniel R. "Boswell, Johnson and a Proverbial Candlestick." Midwestern Journal of Language and Folklore 8 (1982): 120-22.

Reviews the account in the Life of Johnson's severe schoolmaster, Mr. Hawkins, who would, Johnson seems to have told Boswell, beat a boy for not knowing what he could not be expected to know--the Latin for candlestick, for instance. Suggests that Boswell mistakes for fact Johnson's allusion to a seventeenth- and eighteenth-century proverb, "Tace is Latin for a candle," a traditional admonition to keep silent.

259. Dowling, William C. "Solipsism and Despair in the Life of Johnson." Prose Studies 5 (1982): 294-308.

Argues that Johnson's melancholy in the Life--"a gloomy plunge into meaninglessness and despair"--is an "authentication of his heroism": while Johnson as a moralist affirms stability, ontological security, and religious belief, his own experience of spiritual disintegration, ontological anxiety, and radical doubt confirm his heroic status: "the truth affirmed by Johnson in his writings and conversation is a truth won through trial and suffering unknown to lesser souls."

260. Koepp, Robert Charles. "Johnsonian and Boswellian Strains in Early Nineteenth-Century English Biography." Dissertation, University of Wisconsin-Madison, 1982.

Distinguishes between Boswell's scientific, inductive approach to biography and Johnson's deductive, moral, and interpretive theory and practice. Examines Lockhart's Scott and several early lives of Byron as examples of Boswellian biography.

261. Epstein, William H. "Bios and Logos: Boswell's Life of Johnson and Recent Literary Theory." South Atlantic Quarterly 82 (1983): 246-55.

Attributes the dearth of post-structuralist studies of the Life to the complex phenomenon of the Boswell papers, suggesting that their discovery and publication signal a shift of cultural power from Britain to America and a revision of nineteenth-century views of the eighteenth century. Claims that the papers have created at Yale a corporate enterprise producing texts of such variety and complexity that most "consumers" are likely to be bewildered and intimidated. Considers the contrast between the Yale Boswell and the "Yale Mafia"--deconstructionist critics associated with Yale--as representative of the state of modern criticism. Argues that Item 255, though claiming to be a deconstruction of the Life, actually inhabits a "no-man's land" between the formalist and deconstructionist approaches: Dowling's book borrows the language of Derrida, though it displays none of the self-reflexity of a truly deconstructionist study.

262. Rewa, Michael. Reborn as Meaning: Panegyrical Biography from Isocrates to Walton. Washington, D.C.: University Press of America, 1983.

Describes the Life as a fusion of modern empirical biography and classical panegyric, a mode intended to inspire admiration, the rhetoric of praise having been developed by Greek and Roman biographers and employed in saints' lives, Greville's Life of Sir Philip Sidney, and Walton's Life of John Donne.

263. Siebenschuh, William R. Fictional Techniques and Factual Works. Athens: University of Georgia Press, 1983.

Explores the role of literary techniques--dialogue, plot, dramatizations, symbolism, imagery, myth--in factual narratives: Boswell's Life, Newman's Apologia, Gosse's Father and Son, and Gibbon's Decline and Fall. Argues that literary art and factual content may coexist, that techniques associated with fiction "can sometimes be used, without compromising a reader's expectations or a work's generic integrity, to make interpretive factual statements." Suggests that Boswell's artistic choices--for example, his dramatizations, shifts in point of view, allusions--all enhance rather than diminish the value of his interpretative portrait of Johnson. Concludes that ultimately, Boswell is more concerned with the most important truths of Johnson's character than with factual data and that "in biography the opposite of fact is not always fiction, and the opposite of historical truth is not necessarily a lie."

264. Wendorf, Richard. "Ut Pictura Biographia: Biography and Portrait Painting as Sister Arts." Articulate Images: The Sister Arts from Hogarth to Tennyson. Edited by Richard Wendorf. Minneapolis: University of Minnesota Press, 1983. 98-124.

Surveys the parallels between biography and portrait painting in theory and practice with special attention to Dryden, Walton, Jonathan Richardson, Johnson, Reynolds, and Boswell. Notes the common goal of the two arts--to represent an individual subject's character and to reveal general human nature--and the fundamental differences between them: portrait painting is spatial, biography temporal. Believes that even though Boswell's metaphor for the Life as a Flemish painting is well known, his method is most distinctive for his handling of time, not of visual elements.

265. Mathur, R.K. "Dr. Johnson's Contempt for Stage Acting: An Explanation." Prajna 30.1 (1984): 1-8.

Disagrees with Boswell's explanation for Johnson's low opinion of players--"imperfection of his senses," the rejection of his tragedy, and envy of Garrick--and suggests instead that Johnson objected primarily to tragic acting only, because he believed gesture cannot heighten a serious work: a tragedy, he believed, therefore, is best read rather than acted.

266. Riely, John C. "The Biographer as Advocate: Boswell and the 'Supper of Larks' Case." Greene Centennial Studies; Essays Presented to Donald Greene in the Centennial Year of the University of Southern California. Edited by Paul J. Korshin and Robert R. Allen. Charlottesville: University Press of Virginia, 1984. 307-19.

Argues that in his "animadversions" on Piozzi in the Life, Boswell shifts from a judicial to an advocatory role, from being concerned with discovering the truth to being intent on discrediting a rival. Focuses on Piozzi's claim that Johnson responded insensitively to her expression of grief for a cousin killed in America ("...how would the world be worse for it, I may ask, if all your relatives were at once spitted like larks, and dressed for Presto's supper?") and shows that in order to refute her, Boswell relies on a different version obtained through Malone from Baretti, a violent enemy of Piozzi and a man not known for truthfulness, concealing the fact that his case rests on hearsay evidence.

267. Bogel, Fredric V. " 'Did You Once See Johnson Plain?': Reflections on Boswell's Life and the State of Eighteenth-Century Studies." Boswell's Life of Johnson: New Questions, New Answers. Edited by John A. Vance. Athens: University of Georgia Press, 1985. 73-93.

Notes that the central critical debate surrounding the Life remains the source of its greatness, whether truth (Johnson's greatness) or art (Boswell's literary skill), the debate between historical scholarship and New Criticism, between history and poetry. Argues that today those who affirm the historical Johnson and deny Boswell's artistry reveal a naive desire to believe that Johnson--or anyone--can be experienced directly, unmediated, "unmeshed in the web of textuality." Considers the current debate symptomatic of current eighteenth-century criticism, which is torn between an incomplete formalism and an antiliterary historicism. Calls for "an intenser formalism," one that treats factuality and referentiality as conventions of "factual" forms, focuses on interpretation rather than evaluation, and recognizes that questions of fact and art are not about intrinsic qualities but about perspectives from which a text may be viewed.

268. Brady, Frank. "Fictional Techniques in Factual Works." Eighteenth-Century Theory and Interpretation. 26 (1985): 158-70.

Argues that Siebenschuh's discussion of the Life in Item 263 is flawed by misreadings of particular scenes--Johnson's fit of laughter inspired by Langton's will, for example--and by theoretical confusion. Siebenschuh's dichotomy between pleasurable and truthful works, derived from Coleridge via Rader, involves not literary classification but value judgment. Siebenschuh's use of the terms "fact" and "fiction" likewise cloud important issues; more useful is the distinction between invented and remembered narratives. In addition, suggests that Siebenschuh makes unjustified concessions to critics of Boswell such as Greene and Schwartz, who claim that Boswell lacked or concealed important information and misinterpreted what he did possess: Boswell's only significant suppressions were required by eighteenth-century standards of decorum; his interpretation of Johnson, which he was far better qualified to make than twentieth-century scholars, was never questioned by those who knew Johnson well--Hector, William Adams, Malone.

269. Burke, John J., Jr. "But Boswell's Johnson Is Not Boswell's Johnson." Boswell's Life of Johnson: New Questions, New Answers. Edited by John A. Vance. Athens: University of Georgia Press, 1985. 172-203.

Refuses to accept that, in general, human beings are incapable of arriving at objective truth in human affairs, or, in particular, that Boswell's Life presents only "Boswell's Johnson," one subjective version of Johnson, no better than any other version. Shows that Boswell's Johnson is not completely subjective but rather a complex blend of material gathered from a variety of sources: Johnson himself, as well as Reynolds, Hector, William Adams, Garrick, Charles Burney, and, especially Langton. Concludes that Boswell's Life, despite its shortcomings, remains unsurpassed, a magnificent biography, a rich human portrait, remarkably accurate, one that evokes in readers the same affection that Boswell felt for Johnson.

270. Greene, Donald J. "Boswell's Life as 'Literary Biography.' " Boswell's Life of Johnson: New Questions, New Answers. Edited by John A. Vance. Athens: University of Georgia Press, 1985. 161-71.

Reiterates his claims about Boswell's general inaccuracy in light of Pottle's response in Item 235 to his own earlier attacks on Boswell's practice (Items 189 and 245). Focuses on two famous passages: Johnson's remark about Lady Diana Beauclerk ("The woman's a whore, and there's an end on't"), and his "translation" of one of his own remarks ("It has not wit enough to keep it sweet" becomes "It has not vitality enough to preserve it from putrefaction"). Shows that both are of dubious origin: there are no sources in the journal or records by others present that confirm Boswell's version in the Life. Believes that to suggest, as Pottle and Rader do, that Boswell's version in the Life belongs to the genre of literary biography, distinct from merely informative or factual biography, is "a plea to legitimize falsification by biographers." Points once again to modern biographers such as Richard Ellmann who combine exacting scholarship with narrative skill as the proper models for biographical practice, not Boswell.

271. Greene, Donald J. "Samuel Johnson." The Craft of Literary Biography. Edited by Jeffrey Meyers. New York, Schocken, 1985. 9-32.

Argues that a modern biographer of Johnson must distinguish between the facts about him--he was not, for example, prone to speak of himself as Dr. Johnson or to pepper his discourse with "sirs"--and the "cherished myth" of Sam Johnson, amiable eccentric and literary dictator. Suggests that the myth is largely Boswell's invention, a response to his own psychic need to cut his master down to size, an exercise likewise enjoyed by generations of middlebrow readers, pleased to patronize a literary giant. Concludes that a successful biographer must avoid Boswell's errors--lack of proportion, ignorance of important contemporary sources--in order to write a genuine biography--not table talk--that does justice to the enduring significance and complexity of Johnson's thought and writing.

272. Kernan, Alvin B. "The Social Construction of Literature." Kenyon Review 7.4 (1985): 31-46.

Describes the Life as an early celebration of the professional writer as cultural hero, one of "the central statements of what it really meant and felt like to be a hack working in the new Grub Street print business."

273. Newman, Donald J. "The Death Scene and the Art of Suspense in Boswell's Life of Johnson." Boswell's Life of Johnson: New Questions, New Answers. Edited by John A. Vance. Athens: University of Georgia Press, 1985. 53-72.

Defends Boswell from those critics who maintain that the death scene in the Life is disappointing, both biographically and artistically, because it is based on the narrative conventions of holy dying, not on firsthand observation. Describes the scene's two-part structure--drama (the death itself) and exposition (others' accounts)--and argues that the death scene is the climax of the book, the resolution of its central conflict--between Johnson's dread of God's punishment and his belief in God's mercy, between fear and faith. Boswell builds suspense by creating uncertainty about Johnson's death, when it will come and how he will meet it, before calming readers' anxieties with the climactic account of Johnson's resigned and peaceful acceptance of death.

274. Schwartz, Richard B. "The Boswell Problem." Epilogue. Boswell's Life of Johnson: New Questions, New Answers. Edited by John A. Vance. Athens: University of Georgia Press, 1985. 248-59.

Identifies the key issue in "the Boswell problem" as biography's combining art and history. Maintains that as history--as a record of facts--Boswell's Life is inadequate. Readers cannot be satisfied with Boswell's Life as the sole source of information about Johnson, no matter how artful the book is: Johnson is important not simply because his life was "tellable," but because he is an intellectual and moral model. Concludes that Boswell's Life, though a "misleading and inadequate secondary source for the study of Samuel Johnson," must be read, taught, and debated, because it remains one of the essential texts of western culture.

275. Siebenschuh, William R. "Boswell's Second Crop of Memory: A New Look at the Role of Memory in the Life." Boswell's Life of Johnson: New Questions, New Answers. Edited by John A. Vance. Athens: University of Georgia Press, 1985. 94-109.

Examines Boswell's remarkable memory--his ability to reconstruct at a distance of twenty years entire scenes based only on fragmentary notes--in light of current research in the fields of memory and perception. Speculates that the coherent image of Johnson in the Life, traditionally thought to be shaped by Boswell's conscious artistic choices, may be the product of memory, which we now know selects and even "revises." Shows that recent clinical work demonstrates Boswell's ability to record and recall information about Johnson is credible, and that Boswell employed a number of techniques now known to enhance the power of memory: using key words and phrases as cues, associating events with landmark occasions, anchoring conversations in space and time. Suggests that although memory does select and alter what it records, Boswell's portrait of Johnson is not an invention: it is consistent with those of Hawkins and Piozzi, and is the product of a complex interplay among memory, written records, and Boswell's own interests and preoccupations, "the relationship between psychic pressures from the present and explicit data from the past--of the gray area that may have mixed memory and desire."

276. Singh, Brijraj. "Boswell, Johnson, and Wilkes." Rajasthan Studies in English 17 (1985): 108-23.

No library subscribing to the OCLC international data base--including the Library of Congress--reports to have this volume.

277. Spacks, Patricia Meyer. "Biography: Moral and Physical Truth." Gossip. Chicago: University of Chicago Press, 1985. 92-120.

Locates the appeal of biography in "the universal hunger to penetrate other lives" and argues that Boswell's "modes of knowing and telling connect The Life of Samuel Johnson, LL.D., for all its dignity, with gossip." Although Johnson's conversations--combative, focused on ideas--are not gossip, Boswell as narrator constantly invites his readers to dwell on idiosyncratic detail; Boswell's anecdotal dexterity, comic sense, psychic sensitivity--these "embody the biographer's skills" and also "epitomize the gossip's."

278. Vance, John A., ed. Boswell's Life of Johnson: New Questions, New Answers. Athens: University of Georgia Press, 1985.

Contains Items 208, 235, 245, 267, 269, 270, 273, 274, 275, 279, 280, 281.

279. Vance, John A. Introduction. Boswell's Life of Johnson: New Questions, New Answers. Edited by John A. Vance. Athens: University of Georgia Press, 1985. 1-24.

Surveys the criticism of Boswell's Life since 1970 and identifies two major areas of investigation: first, the accuracy of the Life--what is the relationship between Boswell's presentation of Johnson and the historical Johnson?--and, second, the artistry of the Life--what literary techniques does Boswell employ in his narrative?

280. Vance, John A. "The Laughing Johnson and the Shaping of Boswell's Life." Boswell's Life of Johnson: New Questions, New Answers. Edited by John A. Vance. Athens: University of Georgia Press, 1985. 204-27.

Grants that the Johnson in the Life may be in part a creation of Boswell's art but contends that Johnson himself controlled events and protected his privacy by presenting a persona in company: he deliberately made outrageous and provocative statements in order to tease, shock, or surprise his acquaintances. Believes Boswell did not always understand Johnson's deceptive humor and therefore presents many of his opinions and characteristic stances--his contempt for actors, his anti-Scots bias--as if they were serious pronouncements.

281. Woods, Samuel H., Jr. "Boswell's Presentation of Goldsmith: A Reconsideration." Boswell's Life of Johnson: New Questions, New Answers. Edited by John A. Vance. Athens: University of Georgia Press, 1985. 228-47.

Compares Boswell's portrait of Goldsmith in the Life--"a foolish man who wrote extremely well"--with the more sympathetic views of Reynolds, Johnson, and Percy, the contemporaries who knew him best. Argues that Boswell did not understand Goldsmith, that the more accurate interpretation is Reynolds's: Goldsmith frequently played the fool in company intentionally, exercising the same gift for comedy that distinguishes his literary works.

Journal of a Tour to the Hebrides

282. Chapman, R.W. "Cancels in Boswell's Hebrides." Bodleian Quarterly Record, July 1924: 124.

Points out a previously undiscovered cancel in the first edition of Boswell's Hebrides.

283. Birrell, Augustine. "Johnson's 'Journey' and Boswell's 'Journal.' " The Nation and Athenaeum, 9 Aug. 1924: 591-92.

Celebrates Chapman's edition, which brings together Johnson's wise and witty Journey and Boswell's even more entertaining Hebrides.

284. Chapman, R.W. Johnson, Boswell, and Mrs. Piozzi: A Suppressed Passage Restored. London: Oxford University Press, 1929.

Supplies a facsimile and a transcript of a paragraph omitted from the published version of a letter Johnson wrote to Thrale that praises Boswell and his Hebridean journal.

285. Robinson, Frederic W. A Commentary and Questionnaire on a Journal of a Tour to the Hebrides (Boswell). London: N.p., 1929.

Provides an introduction and study questions intended to enhance a student's appreciation of Hebrides.

286. Pottle, Frederick A. "Printer's Copy in the Eighteenth Century." Papers of the Bibliographical Society of America 27 (1933): 65-73.

Describes the printer's copy of Boswell's Hebrides and his method of preparing it from the original journal and supplemental leaves.

287. Mitchell, W. Fraser. "A Reminiscence of Boswell: Lord Gardenstone's Laurencekirk Projects." University of Edinburgh Journal 6 (1933-34): 232-41.

Sketches the life and social views of Francis Garden, Lord Gardenshire, mentioned by Boswell in Hebrides as the man who stocked the inn at Laurencekirk with books.

288. Pottle, Frederick A., and Charles H. Bennett. Preface. Boswell's Journal of a Tour to the Hebrides with Samuel Johnson, LL.D., 1773. Now Published from the Original Manuscript. New York: Viking Press, 1936. vii-xiv.

Explains that this volume--Boswell's journal of his tour with Johnson, as he wrote it in 1773--consists of rough notes made in Edinburgh and two notebooks of fully written entries. Describes

Boswell's extensive revisions, made under the guidance of Malone: he deletes indelicate matter, topographical observation, and personal reflections; he recasts paragraphs and polishes sentences. Suggests that while the published version was indiscreet in its time, the original is more entertaining, fresher, franker, and more intimate than the revised text.

289. Gray, W. Forbes. "Dr. Johnson in Edinburgh." Quarterly Review 269 (1937): 281-97.

Draws on Boswell's Hebrides, Johnson's letters, and contemporaries' reminiscences to review Johnson's activities and opinions while in Edinburgh before and after the trip to the Hebrides. Provides brief biographical sketches of those with whom Johnson conversed: Forbes, Robert Arbuthnot, Andrew Crosbie, and Thomas Blacklock among others.

290. Pearson, Hesketh, and Hugh Kingsmill. Skye High: The Record of a Tour Through Scotland in the Wake of Samuel Johnson and James Boswell. London: Hamish Hamilton, 1937. New York: Oxford University Press, 1938.

Combines commentary on Boswell and Johnson, fresh reflections on topics raised by their books--table manners, friendship, the House of Stuart--and observations of contemporary sights in a narrative, written mainly in the form of a dialogue between the authors.

291. Saunders, Alexander Marion. "In Search of the Landscape: English Travels in the British Isles from 1760 to 1810." Dissertation, Johns Hopkins University, 1937.

Classifies Boswell among those travel writers whose interests lie primarily in people, manners, and domestic economy.

292. Young, G.M. "Boswell--and Unashamed." Daylight and Champaign; Essays. London: Jonathan Cape, 1937. 276-79. Reprint. London: Rupert Hart-Davis, 1948. 260-63.

Reviews Item 288, praising Boswell's "idiomatic ease" and his relish for "the spectacle of human variety."

293. Hazen, Allen T. "Boswell's Cancels in the Tour to the Hebrides." Bibliographical Notes and Queries 2.11 (1938): 7.

Uses a newly discovered letter from Boswell to Thomas Barnard to identify two more cancels in the first edition of Hebrides--leaves C2 and C7.

294. Powell, Lawrence F. "Boswell's Original Journal of His Tour to the Hebrides and the Printed Version." Essays and Studies by Members of the English Association 23 (1938): 58-69.

Describes the numerous changes Boswell made in the original manuscript of the journal of his tour before publication: he polished his sentences, eliminated Scotticisms, and often elevated Johnson's conversation; he omitted detailed descriptions of particular meals, suppressed unflattering references to himself and Sir Alexander MacDonald, and concealed the identity of a number of persons.

295. Robertson, James D. "The Opinions of Eighteenth-Century English Men of Letters Concerning Scotland." Dissertation, University of Cincinnati, 1939.

Draws on Boswell's Hebrides to establish Johnson's views concerning the Scottish people, their customs and institutions.

296. Powell, Lawrence F. "The History of St. Kilda." Review of English Studies 16 (1940): 44-53.

Supports Boswell's assertion in Hebrides that the Reverend Kenneth Macaulay was not the sole author of The History of St. Kilda, that he was assisted by John Macpherson.

297. Powell, Lawrence F. "Boswell's Hebrides, 31 August." Notes and Queries 184 (1943): 202.

Notes that A Treatise Against Drunkenness, a book Boswell found at an inn in Glenmoriston, has not been identified.

298. Powell, Lawrence F. "The Anonymous Designations in Boswell's Journal of a Tour to the Hebrides and Their Identification." Edinburgh Bibliographical Society Transactions 2 (1946): 355-71.

Lists the sixty-four anonymous or general descriptions in Hebrides of people whose real names were known to Boswell; identifies over two-thirds of them.

299. Hetherington, John. The Tour to the Hebrides: Its Value to the Social Historian. Lichfield: Lichfield Johnson Society, 1948.

Praises Johnson's Journey and Boswell's Hebrides as "personal, accurate, and readable records of Highland society in the second half of the eighteenth century," invaluable sources of information on the dying social system of the clans, the transition of the chiefs from patriarchal rulers to rapacious landlords, emigration, Highland hospitality, housing, dress, food, and drink.

300. Watson, Melvin R. "`Momus' and Boswell's Tour." Journal of English and Germanic Philology 48 (1949): 371-74.

Calls attention to a parody of Hebrides published in the essay serial "Momus"; T. Trifler's account of his travels to the Isle of Sky with Nicodemus Humdrum ridicules Boswell's use of trivial anecdotes, his vanity, and his verbosity.

301. Chapman, R.W. "Boswell Without Malone." Johnsonian and Other Essays and Reviews. London: Oxford University Press, 1953. 186-91.

Reviews Item 288 and notes the sort of changes Boswell and Malone made in preparing the text for publication: the deletion of Johnson's coarse language and uncomplimentary remarks about Sir Alexander MacDonald and the revision of Boswell's sentences for greater correctness and elegance.

302. Fletcher, Edward G. "Mrs. Piozzi on Boswell and Johnson's Tour." University of Texas Studies in English 29 (1953): 45-58.

Examines Piozzi's marginalia in her copy of Boswell's Hebrides.

303. McLaren, Moray. The Highland Jaunt: A Study of James Boswell and Samuel Johnson upon their Highland and Hebridean Tour of 1773. New York: William Sloane, 1955.

Retraces Boswell and Johnson's path, combining analysis and appreciation of Boswell's Hebrides and Johnson's Journey with description of the Highlands and Hebrides in the mid-twentieth century.

304. Stucley, Elizabeth F. A Hebridean Journey with Johnson and Boswell. London: Christopher Johnson, 1956.

Describes the author's journey with her son in the footsteps of Boswell and Johnson, visiting the same houses and castles they did, and speaking with many of the descendants of their hosts.

305. Mitchell, Stephen O. "Johnson and Cocker's Arithmetic." Papers of the Bibliographical Society of America 56 (1962): 107-9.

Explains that Boswell finds Johnson's presentation of Cocker's Arithmetic to a Highland girl a cause of merriment because it was an out-of-date textbook, a one-hundred-year-old piece of hack work.

306. Lascelles, Mary. "Notions and Facts: Johnson and Boswell on Their Travels." Johnson, Boswell and Their Circle: Essays Presented to Lawrence Fitzroy Powell in Honour of His Eighty-Fourth Birthday. Oxford: Clarendon Press, 1965. 215-29.

Describes Boswell's proposed responses to the publication of Johnson's Journey, all of which Johnson either discouraged or met with indifference: the immediate publication of his journal in its entirety, the writing of a supplement for publication, the offering of notes to Johnson for the correction of a second edition of the Journey.

307. Skipp, Francis E. "Johnson and Boswell Afloat." New Rambler: Journal of the Johnson Society of London B.16 (1965): 21-28.

Describes Boswell and Johnson's dangerous passage from the Isle of Skye to the Isle of Coll, contrasting Johnson's restrained account in his Journey with Boswell's vivid recreation in Hebrides.

308. Davies, Eileen C. "An Epigram on Boswell." Notes and Queries, n.s. 14 (1967): 182.

Reprints a satiric epigram on Hebrides, first published in Jackson's Oxford Journal, 8 September 1787.

309. Schalit, Ann E. "Literature as Product and Process: Two Differing Accounts of the Same Trip." Serif 4.1 (1967): 10-17.

Characterizes Johnson's Journey as an example of literature as product--formal and controlled--as opposed to Boswell's Hebrides, an example of literature as process--fluid and spontaneous.

310. Pottle, Frederick A. Preface. Boswell's Journal of a Tour to the Hebrides with Samuel Johnson, LL.D., 1773. Edited by Frederick A. Pottle and Charles H. Bennett. New York: McGraw-Hill, 1971. ix-xxviii.

Describes Boswell's journal of his Hebridean tour as "a first-rate travel book" and as "the best of his journals," more detailed and more intimate in its portrayal of Johnson than the heavily edited published version. Explains that this edition supplements Item 288, the 1936 text, with new illustrations, a corrected index, and new notes based on documents recovered since 1936.

311. MacLean, Virginia. Much Entertainment: A Visual and Culinary Record of Johnson and Boswell's Tour of Scotland in 1773. London: Dent; New York: Liveright, 1973.

Illustrates Boswell and Johnson's tour with caricatures, portraits, and landscapes, and provides recipes for some of the meals they were served.

312. Quennell, Peter. " 'Who Can Like the Highlands?' " Horizon 15 (Spring, 1973): 89-102.

Traces Boswell and Johnson's travels in the Highlands, based on Johnson's Journey, Boswell's original journal, and his published Hebrides. Includes maps, photographs of Scottish sites, and reproductions of Rowlandson's engravings.

313. Steinberg, Theodore L. "J & B: Learning to Love the Scotch." New Rambler: Journal of the Johnson Society of London 15 (1974): 23-29.

Studies the reception of Johnson's Journey and Boswell's Hebrides: Johnson's book received a favorable popular response but a mixed critical reaction, a number of reviewers objecting to his discussion of Ossian and of Highland "credulity"; Boswell, though his book enjoyed spectacular sales, was criticized by some reviewers for his indiscretion, insulted in the private correspondence of those he depicted unfavorably, and ridiculed in the engravings of Thomas Rowlandson and the poetry of Peter Pindar (Dr. John Walcot).

314. Riely, John C. and Alvaro Ribeiro. " 'Mrs. Thrale' in the Tour: A Boswellian Puzzle." Papers of the Bibliographical Society of America 69 (1975): 151-63.

Reviews the controversy surrounding Johnson's pronouncement on Elizabeth Montagu's Essay on the Writings and Genius of Shakespeare ("...neither I, nor Beauclerk, nor Mrs. Thrale, could get through it"), focusing on whether or not Boswell, as he claimed, did indeed strike out Thrale's name in the proof sheet only to restore it after two to three hundred copies had been printed. Notes that not a single copy has been discovered in this first state and hypothesizes that Boswell was mistaken and that the name was restored before any copies were printed.

315. Kay, Donald. "Purposeful Contrarieties in Boswell's Tour to the Hebrides and in Johnson's Journey to the Western Islands." Aevum 50 (1976): 588-96.

Characterizes Boswell's Hebrides and Johnson's Journey as complementary, noting that Boswell would not have deleted material previously published in Johnson's account had he not wished the two books to be read together. Compares their methods and goals as travel writers: Boswell's focus is biographical, his organization chronological, and his style simple and conversational; Johnson's focus is cultural analysis and moral instruction, his organization topographical, and his style ornate and literary.

316. Lustig, Irma S. "The Compiler of Dr. Johnson's Table Talk, 1785." Papers of the Bibliographical Society of America 71 (1977): 83-88.

Identifies David Evans Macdonnel as the compiler of Dr. Johnson's Table Talk, an unauthorized book of extracts from Boswell's Hebrides published by George Robinson.

317. Meier, T.K. "Johnson and Boswell; On the Survival of Culture." Aberdeen University Review 47 (1978): 329-33.

Analyzes Boswell's Hebrides and Johnson's Journey as contrasting commentaries upon the dying Highland culture and the emergence of a modern commercial society: Johnson, perhaps because of his middle-class background, feels an urge to reform; his approach is historical and institutional, his goal to generalize and unify. Boswell, more aristocratic in outlook, is concerned not so much with the future as with the present moment, not so much devoted to historical generalizations as preserving the peculiarities of individual characters, more interested in private than public morality and welfare.

318. Ogu, Julius Nwuju. "Two Perceptions of One Trip: Samuel Johnson's Journey to the Western Islands of Scotland and James Boswell's Journal of a Tour to the Hebrides with Samuel Johnson, LL.D." Dissertation, Howard University, 1978.

Examines how differences in genre, purpose, method, and, especially, differences in personality, experience, and modes of perception contribute to differences in Johnson's rationalistic and Boswell's romantic accounts of their trip to the Hebrides.

319. Goyette, E. Matthew. "Boswell's Changing Conceptions of His Journal of a Tour to the Hebrides." Papers of the Bibliographical Society of America 73 (1979): 305-14.

Disagrees with Pottle's assertion that Boswell's Hebrides evolved "from a topographical travel book to an authentic transcript to the final, heavily edited conversational journal." Argues instead that Boswell's fragmentary topographical account is in fact part of a narrative supplement to Johnson's Journey, written in 1775 and later incorporated in the 1785 Hebrides. Suggests that Boswell's second and final conception of the journal--as a prelude to the Life, notable for its accuracy and authenticity--crystallized after Johnson's death and remained unchanged through the revision and publication of the manuscript.

320. Wilson, Ross E. "House Building on Coll and Tiree." New Rambler: Journal of the Johnson Society of London 20 (1979): 30-32.

Attributes the architectural superiority of Coll's domestic dwellings at the time of Boswell and Johnson's visit to its history of resident landlords.

321. Housum, Mary E. "Boswell's Account of Bonnie Prince Charlie and the Journal of a Tour to the Hebrides." Studies in Scottish Literature 16 (1981): 135-47.

Considers Boswell's account of Prince Charlie not as digression, as most critics view it, but as an essential part of a book that is a prelude to a biography, a kind of advertisement: along with remarks on the art of biography and passages concerning famous men such as Hume and Garrick, this episode is intended to demonstrate Boswell's skill as a biographer, his regard for authenticity and for domestic detail.

322. McGowan, I.D. "The Making of Boswell's The Journal of a Tour to the Hebrides, 1773-1786." Dissertation, University of Stirling, 1981.

This dissertation is not available from University Microfilms International and does not circulate.

323. Finney, Brian. "Boswell's Hebridean Journal and the Ordeal of Dr. Johnson." Biography 5 (1982): 319-34.

Examines the ways in which Boswell's Hebridean journal, much of which Johnson read, served as "a special channel of communication" between the two men: Boswell disagrees with Johnson, criticizes him, expresses his admiration and affection for him, confesses to him his weakness for women and alcohol, and reveals his intention to write his life. Believes that Boswell and Johnson's disciple-master relationship develops during the course of their travels--with the journal itself "an active ingredient" in the transformation--into a true friendship based on mutual respect and understanding, honesty, and love.

324. Shenker, Israel. In the Footsteps of Johnson and Boswell. New York: Oxford University Press, 1982.

Retraces the journey of Boswell and Johnson through the Highlands and Hebrides, revisiting the landmarks they describe and noting the effects of modernization.

325. Bronson, Bertrand H. "Johnson, Travelling Companion, in Fancy and Fact." Johnson and His Age. Edited by James Engell. Harvard English Studies 12. Cambridge: Harvard University Press, 1984. 163-87.

Compares Imlac, Johnson's alter ego in Rasselas, with Johnson himself as portrayed in Boswell's Hebrides and his own Journey. Describes both as observant, sympathetic, and imaginative traveling companions who find "a partial and temporary alleviation of unhappiness" by embracing new experience.

An Account of Corsica

326. Stobart, M.A. "Boswell in Corsica: The Perfect Journalist on His Travels." Pall Mall Magazine 25 (Oct. 1901): 225-35.

Provides an illustrated account of Boswell's travels in Corsica.

327. Bradley, Rose M. "Boswell and a Corsican Patriot." Nineteenth Century 67 (1910): 130-45.

Describes Boswell's experience in Corsica and sketches the career of Paoli.

328. Tinker, Chauncey B. "A New Nation." Nature's Simple Plan. Princeton: Princeton University Press, 1922. Esp. 48-53.

Treats Boswell's interest in Corsica, inspired by Rousseau, and his celebration of Corsican liberty, equality, and patriotism in his Corsica as representative of eighteenth-century England's fascination with a state of nature and the virtues of a simple, uncivilized life.

329. Bracy, Robert. "Corsica Boswell." Eighteenth-Century Studies. Oxford: Blackwell, 1925. 28-36.

Praises Boswell's Corsica as "one of the most delightful travel-books in our language."

330. Pottle, Frederick A. "Boswell's Corsica." Yale University Library Gazette 1 (1927): 21-22.

Describes two translations of Boswell's Corsica--one Italian, the other Dutch--acquired by Yale.

331. Foladare, Joseph. "James Boswell and Corsica." Dissertation, Yale University, 1936.

Examines Boswell's method of writing Corsica--note-taking, sources, organization--and its critical reception as well as the political effects of Boswell's efforts on behalf of the Corsicans. Includes an annotated edition of Corsica.

332. Corrigan, Beatrice. "Guerrazzi, Boswell, and Corsica." Italica 35 (1958): 25-37.

Traces the influence of Boswell's Corsica on the nineteenth-century novelist Francesco Domenico Guerrazzi and his historical novel Pasquale Paoli (1860).

333. Dilworth, E.N. "Boswell in America." Notes and Queries, n.s. 5 (1958): 220.

Notes the publication of a feature in Bickerstaff's Boston Almanack of 1769 consisting of a biographical sketch of Paoli and a brief extract from Boswell's Corsica.

334. Day, Douglas. "Boswell, Corsica, and Paoli." English Studies 45 (1964): 1-20.

Reviews the political history of Corsica and describes Boswell's friendship with Paoli, the composition and publication of Corsica, and Boswell's efforts to advance the Corsican cause in Great Britain.

335. McLaren, Moray. Corsica Boswell: Paoli, Johnson and Freedom. London: Secker and Warburg, 1966.

Combines an appreciation of Boswell's Corsica, background on Paoli, and description of modern Corsica in an account of the author's travels in Boswell's footsteps.

336. Letzring, Monica. "Mickle, Boswell, Liberty, and the 'Prospects of Liberty and of Slavery.' " Modern Language Review 69 (1974): 489-500.

Examines the correspondence and circumstances surrounding the composition of William Julius Mickle's unfinished poem "Prospects of Liberty and of Slavery": Boswell agreed to read a tragedy by Mickle and to recommend it to Garrick; in return, Mickle's "Prospects" was to include lines complimenting Boswell and supporting Paoli and the Corsican struggle for independence.

337. Carnie, Robert H. "Boswell's Account of Corsica 1768." The Book Collector 26 (1977): 186-94.

Provides a bibliographical account of the first edition of Corsica, showing that though printed in Glasgow, the book has an Edinburgh cancel.

338. Foladare, Joseph. Boswell's Paoli. Transactions of the Connecticut Academy of Arts and Sciences, 48. Hamden, CT: Archon Books for the Connecticut Academy of Arts and Sciences, 1979.

Draws on Boswell's hitherto unpublished letters, journals, and manuscripts to provide a full portrait of Paoli and narrative of his life, more objective than Boswell's and more accurate than those of previous biographers.

339. Frings, Emma Jane. "James Boswell and the Heroic Ideal: A Study of the 'Corsican Journals and Memoirs' and the 'Private Journals.' " Dissertation, Northern Illinois University, 1979.

Argues that Boswell's portrayal of Paoli exemplifies his heroic ideal--a confident public leader--an ideal that Boswell measures himself against in the journals. Points out the fictional conventions Boswell employs in Corsica: Boswell as protagonist, a narrative frame--a quest for greatness--dramatic scenes, and dialogue.

340. Brodwin, Stanley. " 'Old Plutarch at Auchinleck': Boswell's Muse of Corsica." Philological Quarterly 62 (1983): 69-93.

Analyzes Boswell's debt to Plutarch in Corsica. Boswell not only imitates Plutarchian methods--a moral focus, reliance on anecdote, a lack of attention paid the subject's influence--he also embraces Plutarchian values: moral beauty--the virtues of moderation, courage, wisdom, and justice--realized in political action. In addition, Boswell finds in Plutarchian biography the means to integrate conflicting radical and conservative demands: Paoli embodies both Rousseau's love of liberty and of the natural and Johnson's "tough-minded political realism."

341. Vivies, Jean. "Boswell, Smollett, and Corsica: A Note." Notes and Queries 31 (1984): 401-2.

Points out that Boswell in Corsica notes two errors in Smollett's History of England concerning Paoli and the Corsican rebels; upon learning that Smollett was offended, Boswell wrote to him, explaining that he meant only to correct the errors, not to impeach the author, and thanking him for his "generous warmth in favor of the Corsicans."

342. "Thoughts on Family and Friends: Some Little Known Anecdotes and Random Reflections by James Boswell." Bookman's Journal 12 (May 1925): 37-46.

Excerpts anecdotes from Boswell's notebooks.

343. Batty, W.R. "Boswell's Shorthand." Times Literary Supplement, 4 Aug. 1932: 557.

Suggests that Boswell's shorthand was intended not to expedite his handwriting but to conceal his meaning.

344. Pottle, Frederick A. "Boswell's Shorthand." Times Literary Supplement, 28 July 1932: 545.

Describes a cryptic alphabet used by Boswell in the early journals.

345. Kirwan, H.N. "The Boswell Supplement." London Mercury 27 (1933): 331-40.

Suggests that Boswell's greatness as journalist lies in his passion for truth, his willingness to reveal "the shameful secrets of his soul"--what most men and women conceal not only from others but also from themselves.

346. Warnock, Robert. "Boswell in Italy." Dissertation, Yale University, 1933.

This dissertation is not available from University Microfilms International and does not circulate.

347. Esdaile, Arundell. "Boswell in His Diaries." Library Association Record (Feb. 1934): 34-40. Reprint. Autolycus' Pack and Other Light Wares: Being Essays, Addresses, and Verses. London: Grafton, 1940. 74-92.

Surveys Boswell's private papers, a diary comparable to Pepys's in its objectivity, fullness, and vitality. Considers Boswell's romanticism, melancholy, and ambition, describes his interviews with Rousseau, Voltaire, and Hume, and his marriage to Margaret Montgomerie, and briefly examines Boswell's expansion of his notes into a scene from the Life.

348. Reeves, A.S. Frere. "Boswell's Journal." Times Literary Supplement, 14 Nov. 1936: 928.

Explains the plan of publication of the Boswell papers by Viking and William Heinemann.

349. Pottle, Frederick A. "Queries from Boswell." Notes and Queries 175 (1938): 208.

Asks for the source of three quotations from Boswell's "Journal of My Jaunt, Harvest, 1762" and from the German journal.

350. Warnock, Robert. "Boswell and Bishop Trail." Notes and Queries 174 (1938): 44-45.

Reconstructs Boswell's conversations with Bishop Trail, a Scotsman he met in Florence in 1765.

351. Pottle, Frederick A. "A Blank in Boswell's Journal." Notes and Queries 177 (1939): 80.

Seeks assistance in identifying a word left out of Boswell's journal entry for 10 August 1774.

352. Murray, John. "Boswell in Edinburgh." Dissertation, Yale University, 1939.

This dissertation is not available from University Microfilms International and does not circulate.

353. Senex [Horatio Townsend]. "A Blank in Boswell's Journal." Notes and Queries 177 (1939): 319-320.

Speculates that the word left out of Boswell's journal entry for 10 August 1774 is "perspective." See Item 351.

354. Letts, M. "Boswell's Journal: Source of Quotation Wanted." Notes and Queries 178 (1940): 89.

Replies to Item 355, suggesting Measure for Measure, II, ii.

355. Pottle, Frederick A. "Boswell's Journal: Source of Quotation Wanted." Notes and Queries 178 (1940): 44.

Seeks the source of a passage quoted in the journal on 7 November 1775.

356. Warnock, Robert. "Boswell on the Grand Tour." Studies in Philology 39 (1942): 650-661.

Reviews Boswell's activities in Italy in 1765: his sightseeing and study of the fine arts, his "amourous intrigues," and his acquaintance with Wilkes, Lord Monstuart, and Andrew Lumisden.

357. Abbott, Claude C. "Boswell: The Robert Spence Watson Memorial Lecture for 1945-1946." Newcastle-Upon-Tyne: Literary and Philosophical Society, 1946.

Traces the discovery of Boswell's journals and shows that they reveal both his attractive personal qualities--good humor, zest for life, curiosity about human nature--and his skill as a writer--honesty, a remarkable memory, a Wordsworthian ability to recreate a particular moment, and a vigorous style.

358. Tinker, Chauncey B. "The Great Diarist, and Some Others." Essays in Retrospect. New Haven: Yale University Press, 1948. 16-18.

Suggests that Boswell shared with Pepys a "relish for existence," a "mania" for collecting and preserving both physical relics and the details of experience, and a respect for factual accuracy.

359. Abbott, Claude C. "New Light on Johnson and Boswell." The Listener, 19 May 1949: 853-54.

Asserts that twentieth-century scholarship emphatically establishes Boswell as "a man and a writer interesting and valuable for his own sake," his most remarkable achievement his thirty-three-year journal.

360. Pottle, Frederick A. "James Boswell, Journalist." The Age of Johnson: Essays Presented to Chauncey Brewster Tinker. Edited by Frederick W. Hilles. New Haven: Yale University Press, 1949. 15-25.

Considers Boswell's journals his "primary literary achievement," and the source of the Life's unique appeal, the conversations, which are the product of literary methods--individuation of speakers, the use of stage directions, the casting of dialogue in dramatic form--Boswell began to practice and refine in his journals before even meeting Johnson. Suggests that Boswell may have learned "the power of dialogue and the virtue of gesture" from Sterne and Fielding, whose work he admired and became acquainted with before the inception of his journal.

361. Spalding, P.A. Self-Harvest: A Study of Diaries and the Diarist. London: Independent Press, Ltd., 1949. 36-38, 84-87.

Considers Boswell's belief that an individual should live no more than he or she can record the best statement of the diarist's impulse to preserve each experience not for any utilitarian value but for its own sake. Calls Boswell's journal "a diary as remarkable as Pepys's."

362. Auden, W.H. "Young Boswell." New Yorker, 25 Nov. 1950: 134-36.

Reviews Boswell's London Journal, describing it as a remarkably unself-conscious self-portrait; Boswell's presentation of himself is "complete and transparent." Characterizes Boswell as "a thoroughly ordinary man"; readers imagine themselves thinking and behaving in much the same way as Boswell does, thus, "in reading Boswell each of us is confronted by himself."

363. Pottle, Frederick A. Introduction. Boswell's London Journal, 1762-1763. Now First Published from the Original Manuscript. The Yale Editions of the Private Papers of James Boswell. Edited by Frederick A. Pottle. New York: McGraw-Hill, 1950. 1-37.

Sketches Boswell's life up to 1762--his education, his relationship with his father, his friends, his attraction to London--and describes London life in the eighteenth century--transportation, lodgings, coffee-houses and taverns, the theater. Explains that this journal is "the most carefully and elaborately written of all Boswell's journals"; the leisure he had to write and his method of posting his journal at intervals allow him to artfully shape his material, to select significant details, and to heighten suspense. Concludes that Boswell, though lacking invention, was "a great imaginative artist," combining the frankness of Pepys and the self-analytic skill of Rousseau.

364. Lindsay, Norman A.W. "The New Boswell." Bulletin 72 (Feb. 1951): 2.

Describes Boswell's London Journal, like Pepys's Diary, as a "masterpiece of self-revelation," though far more self-conscious and theatrical.

365. Pottle, Frederick A. Introduction. Boswell in Holland 1762-1764. The Yale Editions of the Private Papers of James Boswell. Edited by Frederick A. Pottle. New York: McGraw-Hill, 1952. ix-xix.

Explains that Boswell's Dutch journal, from August 1763 to June 1764, was lost in his lifetime, and that this volume is comprised of miscellaneous documents--daily memoranda, letters, verses, language exercises--arranged in chronological order. Suggests that this compilation, though of less literary merit than Boswell's fully written journal, does give a better general impression of the collection of Boswell's papers, and may reveal more about the private Boswell, during this period heroically virtuous but miserable.

366. Pottle, Frederick A., ed. "Boswell in Love: His Private Papers and Correspondence with Zélide." Atlantic Monthly, Apr. 1952: 34-43.

Introduces and selects documents from Boswell in Holland, focusing on Boswell's relationship with Zélide.

367. Probstein, Inge. "Boswell's London Journal, 1778." Dissertation, Yale University, 1952.

This dissertation is not available from University Microfilms International and does not circulate.

368. Yoklavich, J. "Hamlet in Shammy Shoes." Shakespeare Quarterly 3 (July 1952): 209-18.

Cites a passage in Boswell's London Journal as evidence that Thomas Sheridan was the first to view the character of Hamlet as "intellectual and irresolute."

369. Pottle, Frederick A., Introduction. Boswell on the Grand Tour: Germany and Switzerland, 1764. The Yale Editions of the Private Papers of James Boswell. Edited by Frederick A. Pottle. New York: McGraw-Hill, 1953.

Describes the contents of this volume: neither a continuous, polished book-length manuscript like Boswell's London Journal nor a chronological mosaic like Boswell in Holland, it contains Boswell's entire journal for the period with a number of important letters and other documents inserted "to round out the narrative or to vary it pleasingly." Notes that Boswell at this time is "almost continuously happy," convinced finally that he need not make himself over into Johnson or Digges but rather to be himself: "a citizen of the world, exhibiting the infinite resources of his own versatile and original spirit." Considers Boswell's records of his conversations with Rousseau and Voltaire evidence of his comic genius; he is both "minutely attentive" and "heroically unaware."

370. Pritchett, V.S. "Boswell's London." Books in General. New York: Harcourt, Brace, 1953. 75-80.

Suggests that as a young man in London, released from a severe Presbyterian upbringing, Boswell experiences life as a hallucination--vivid and surprising. Notes that the London Journal, though seemingly transparent, is in fact artfully fashioned, informed by Boswell's foreknowledge of events as he posted his journal.

371. Brady, Frank. Introduction. Boswell on the Grand Tour: Italy, Corsica, and France, 1765-1766. The Yale Editions of the Private Papers of James Boswell. Edited by Frank Brady and Frederick A. Pottle. New York: McGraw-Hill, 1955. ix-xxv.

Shows that in this volume consisting of rough notes and memoranda, letters and fully written journals, and part of Corsica, Boswell focuses primarily on three subjects: sex, religion, and politics. Boswell documents his quest for sexual experience--his most notable conquest was Girolama Piccolomini, the wife of the mayor of Sienna--and attempts to discover whether he is a libertine or faithful lover. In addition, Boswell searches for "a solid religious foundation" but finds neither certainty nor a means to reconcile his conduct with his principles. Finally, he attempts to acquire a position through the political influence of his friends Wilkes and Lord Mountstuart, before finding in Paoli and Corsica a new hero and a cause.

372. Denvir, Bernard. "Guillaume Martin." Times Literary Supplement, 4 Nov. 1955: 657.

Identifies a French painter mentioned in Item 371.

373. Brady, Frank. Introduction. Boswell in Search of a Wife, 1766-1769. The Yale Editions of the Private Papers of James Boswell. Edited by Frank Brady and Frederick A. Pottle. New York: McGraw-Hill, 1956. ix-xxvi.

Characterizes 1766-69 as Boswell's "marvelous years," when he reached his greatest maturity, became a lawyer, achieved literary renown with the publication of Corsica, and, after courting a number of candidates, married Margaret Montgomerie, "the woman who best suited him." Notes that Boswell's prose displays "the extraordinary expressiveness of the great writer": the journal is an engaging mixture of description and narration; packed with significant detail; simple, vital, and clear--"a triumph of the normal vision."

374. "Conversations with Rousseau." Saturday Review of Literature, 3 Oct. 1956: 15-16.

Excerpts Item 369.

375. Esdaile, Arundell and Edmund Esdaile. "Boswell on the Grand Tour." Quarterly Review 294 (Oct. 1956): 464-74.

Traces Boswell's travels through Holland, Germany, Switzerland, Italy, Corsica, and France. Emphasizes the personal qualities--charm, affability, versatility--that made Boswell a good traveler and won him the acquaintance of Voltaire, Rousseau, and Paoli.

376. Sheldon, Esther K. "Boswell's English in the London Journal." PMLA 71 (1956): 1067-93.

Examines Boswell's language in the London Journal in light of the standards of correctness established by the grammarians of the eighteenth century. Finds that Boswell's writing frequently does not conform to the rules concerning agreement, parallelism, the subjunctive mood, pronoun reference, tense consistency, and usage, confirming modern linguists' belief that such grammatical rules bore little relation to actual usage.

377. Roberts, S.C. "Pepys and Boswell." Dr. Johnson and Others. Cambridge: Cambridge University Press, 1958. 24-39.

Argues that despite the obvious differences between Pepys's neat ten-year diary and Boswell's vast record of journals, letters, and memoranda written over forty years, both men possessed a willingness to record their least credible features, a zest for life, an appetite for pleasure, and tremendous personal charm.

378. Nolan, Paul T. "A Shakespeare Idol in America." Mississippi Quarterly 12 (1959): 64-74.

Compares Boswell's views on Shakespeare recorded in his London Journal with those made by the American playwright Espy Williams (1852-1908) in his journal in order to establish that the idolatry of Shakespeare was a nineteenth-century American phenomenon.

379. Wimsatt, William K., Jr. "James Boswell: The Man and His Journal." Yale Review 49 (1959): 80-92.

Revised and reprinted as Item 391.

380. Wimsatt, William K., Jr. Introduction. Boswell for the Defence, 1769-1774. The Yale Editions of the Private Papers of James Boswell. Edited by William K. Wimsatt, Jr., and Frederick A. Pottle. New York: McGraw-Hill, 1959. ix-xxix.

Notes that Boswell's journal for this period shows "the maturing effects of a prudent marriage" slowly giving way to "more radical impulses of extravagance." He is at first a model husband, an industrious advocate, and a dutiful son. By 1773, however, Boswell's dark side re-emerges--depression, heavy drinking, differences with his father. Suggests that the fascination of Boswell's journal is the result of his following so faithfully Johnson's advice to record "the state of your own mind": he records his joy and his madness, his quiet pleasures and his gross intemperances, all the oppositions of his character, always realistically. Believes that Boswell "projects himself as a figure of unique fictive significance," like an eighteenth-century sentimental hero, portrayed as vividly and eliciting responses as powerful and complex as any invented character.

381. Phillipson, John S. "Boswell Rediscovered--A Decade Later." Catholic Library World (May 1960): 491-96, 539.

Reviews the events of Boswell's life recorded in the first five volumes of the trade edition of the private papers and suggests that their publication compels a reappraisal of Boswell: rather than being the hack or toady he has been portrayed as, Boswell may prove to be "one of the major prose writers of the eighteenth century."

382. Huseboe, Arthur R. "Boswell's Broken Resolutions." North Dakota Quarterly 29 (1961): 42-45.

Summarizes the resolutions Boswell recorded in the London Journal, those he kept (to keep a journal, to practice frugality) and those he broke (to be reserved and dignified, to avoid debauchery, to attend church services regularly).

383. Morgan, H.A. "Boswell on the Grand Tour." New Rambler: Journal of the Johnson Society of London, June 1961: 14-19.

Reviews the most memorable incidents on Boswell's journey through Europe from 1763 to 1766, especially his interviews with Rousseau and Voltaire, claiming that in the course of his travels, Boswell discovered the danger of imitating great men and the necessity of embracing and accepting his own unique character.

384. Fussell, Paul. "The Force of Literary Memory in Boswell's London Journal." Studies in English Literature 2 (1962): 351-57.

Illustrates how in the London Journal, Boswell draws on favorite literary texts--the Spectator, The Beggar's Opera, Farquhar's Recruiting Officer--in order "to lend either a heroic or sophisticated dimension to his existence" and how he employs literary models from Hamlet to Gulliver's Travels in his shaping of particular scenes. Notes Boswell's particular fondness for dramatic literature and the theater, and his tendency to view his own life "as an accumulation of scenes from tragedy, sentimental comedy, and farce."

385. Kiley, Frederick S. "Boswell's Literary Art in the London Journal." College English 23 (1962): 629-32.

Describes the London Journal as "a ritual of rejuvenation": Boswell seeks independence from his father in the underworld of London, where he experiences disillusionment, disappointment, and fear before achieving a measure of self-knowledge and psychic balance through his friendship with Johnson, his substitute father. Boswell's artistry lies in his ability to shape the facts of his life into a satisfying narrative structure in which every part contributes to the overall design.

386. Pottle, Frederick A. "The Yale Editions of the Private Papers of James Boswell." Ventures 2 (1963): 11-15.

Reviews the first thirteen years of operation of the Yale Editions of the Private Papers of James Boswell and argues that the tremendous popular success of the first volume, Boswell's London Journal, is due only in part to its sensational nature: it was a bestseller in 1950 primarily because Boswell is "a great modern writer," closer in style and outlook to Joyce and Hemingway than Smollett.

387. Ryscamp, Charles. Introduction. Boswell: The Ominous Years, 1774-1776. The Yale Editions of the Private Papers of James Boswell. Edited by Charles Ryscamp and Frederick A. Pottle. New York: McGraw-Hill, 1963. ix-xxiv.

Explains that this portion of Boswell's journals is marked by anxiety, confusion, and occasional despair; it records the central contradictions and complexities of Boswell's character: his piety and his sensual indulgence, his vivacity and his depression, his self-absorption and his compassion. Calls attention to the most memorable episodes of this journal: a threatened duel; a rich London journal, including the famous dinner with Wilkes and Johnson at Dilly's; Boswell's interview with the infamous Margaret Caroline Rudd.

388. Tillinghast, Anthony J. "Boswell Playing a Part." Renaissance & Modern Studies 9 (1965): 86-97.

Notes that critics have described two kinds of role-playing in the journals: Boswell's attempts to be someone else (Addison, Johnson, his father) and his recognition that he sometimes was someone else (advocate, author, laird) as he met various social demands. Suggests that Boswell played a third kind of role, "more obviously histrionic" than the others, intended to reconcile two conflicting roles--say, scholar and man of pleasure--by hiding one and masquerading in the other. Describes role and style in Boswell's journals as interdependent: each role is dramatized, drawing on different literary techniques.

389. Jaarsma, Richard J. "Boswell the Novelist: Structural Rhythms in the London Journal." North Dakota Quarterly 34 (1966): 51-60.

Argues that in the London Journal, Boswell employs dramatic irony and shifts in point of view from actor to observer in order to develop a novelistic theme and structure: Boswell's never-ending quest for happiness, portrayed through a series of carefully arranged scenes--his affair with Louisa, friendship with Johnson, quest for a commission in the Guards--that alternatively emphasize innocence and experience, hope and despair, intellect and passion.

390. Morris, John N. "James Boswell." Versions of the Self: Studies in English Autobiography from John Bunyan to John Stuart Mill. New York: Basic Books, 1966. 169-210.

Places Boswell in the tradition of English autobiography that focuses on private, inward experience and seeks to create "a memorable life" and "a various but coherent self." Argues that Boswell shares the modern beliefs that reality consists of "the data of consciousness" and that literature is a process rather than a product: in the journals, he seeks to record the sequence of ideas and feelings that constitute his experience. Suggests further that Boswell expresses modern anxiety and insecurity about identity and that the journal, the record of his role-playing, is an attempt to create himself, an ultimately unsuccessful attempt to forge a coherent self through literary means.

391. Wimsatt, William K., Jr. "The Fact Imagined: James Boswell." Hateful Contraries: Studies in Literature and Criticism. Lexington: University of Kentucky Press, 1966. 165-83.

Argues that in the journals, Boswell imbues historical fact with universal, symbolic interest; readers respond to the Boswell of the journals as they do a fictional character: he is a figure of "fictive significance"--whether or not he is likable is irrelevant. Boswell's genius is his ability to find the human significance of a scene, to record speech, and to write with effortless immediacy--his gift is "for saying things straight." Suggests that what is most remarkable about the journal is Boswell's ability to entertain opposites--good and evil, prudence and rashness, delight and woe--in his portrayal of life as tragi-comedy.

392. Anderson, Patrick. " 'Cry Like a Parrot, Chatter Like an Ape': James Boswell in Europe." Over the Alps: Reflections on Travel and Travel Writing, with Special Reference to the Grand Tours of Boswell, Beckford, and Byron. London: Hart-Davis, 1969. 45-72.

Surveys Boswell's travels from August 1763 to February 1766 in Holland, Germany, Switzerland, France, Italy, and Corsica. Describes Boswell as a ruthlessly honest traveler, both an egotist and a passionate student of human nature, good-humored, brilliantly accurate and detailed in his observations. Notes that Boswell viewed travel as a means to transform himself: he sought "to grow up, to prove himself strong and manly and...to achieve a balanced, consistent character."

393. Weis, Charles, McC. and Frederick A. Pottle. Introduction. Boswell in Extremes, 1776-1778. The Yale Editions of the Private Papers of James Boswell. Edited by Charles McC. Weis and Frederick A. Pottle. New York: McGraw-Hill, 1970. ix-xxviii.

Notes that these years are marked by Boswell's inner turmoil, his alternating depression and joy, dullness and vigor, degradation and glory. Notes that this volume includes the London journal of 1778, the longest of Boswell's London journals after 1762-63, composed while Boswell was abstaining from alcohol. Suggests that Boswell's melancholy was caused by frustrated ambition, routine, and deep religious and philosophic doubts, which were relieved not at all by his last interview with Hume, also found in this volume.

394. Cushner, Arnold William. "The Imaginative Composition of James Boswell's Grand Tour Journal." Dissertation, Case Western Reserve University, 1972.

Compares Boswell's Grand Tour Journal to similar accounts by Addison, Fielding, and Sterne, and analyzes Boswell's use of narrative conventions--point of view, plot, episode, and character. Considers the journey in this narrative of Boswell, the youthful protagonist, to be from innocence to experience and from ignorance to knowledge.

395. Bell, Robert H. " 'The Blessed Rage for Order': Studies in Autobiography from Bunyan to Boswell." Dissertation, Harvard University, 1972.

This dissertation is not available from University Microfilms International and does not circulate.

396. Primeau, Ronald. "Boswell's 'Romantic Imagination' in the London Journal." Papers on Language and Literature 9 (1973): 15-27.

Finds in Boswell's London Journal a sensibility similar to Wordsworth's: like Wordsworth, Boswell reflects on and celebrates his own imaginative powers, emphasizes "the creative function of imagination," the ability to store his mind with pleasing recollections, and is disappointed when experience fails to meet his imaginative expectations. Shows that Boswell saw his creative imagination as both valuable--it heightened the intensity of pleasing experience--and dangerous--it likewise intensified his unhappiness--and suggests that under Johnson's influence, Boswell came to distrust and seek to restrain it.

397. Grout, Earl Leroy, III. "The Literary Nature of Boswell's Journals." Dissertation, University of Washington, 1974.

Places Boswell's journals in the tradition of the diary in the eighteenth century as a tool for self-improvement and self-discovery. Analyzes how Boswell shaped the journals for various audiences--himself, friends, the public--employed novelistic techniques, and portrayed himself as a hero of sensibility.

398. Spacks, Patricia Meyer. "Laws of Time: Fielding and Boswell." Imagining a Self: Autobiography and the Novel in Eighteenth-Century England. Cambridge: Harvard University Press, 1976. 264-99.

Argues that Boswell's journals assembled as Boswell for the Defence, like Fielding's Amelia, "dramatize the increasing tensions of the effort to preserve selfhood in maturity." Asserts that as Boswell ages, he focuses more on time: he imaginatively reconstructs the past in order to reconstitute himself and a more reassuring world, and he is likewise conscious of the future, the possibility of growth, which he attempts to affirm, and the inevitability of decay, failure, and death, which he reluctantly recognizes.

399. Spacks, Patricia Meyer. "Young Men's Fancies: James Boswell, Henry Fielding." Imagining a Self: Autobiography and the Novel in Eighteenth-Century England. Cambridge: Harvard University Press, 1976. 227-63.

Explores the relationship between imagination and life in Boswell's London Journal and Fielding's Tom Jones: Boswell, who lives life in order to record it and so adjust his character by consulting the mirror of his journal, like Tom Jones, is a young man who must invent himself and discover his place in the world. Describes the journal as Boswell's "artificial memory," a work of imagination, and the instrument of his achieving a reconciliation of imagination and reason and his attaining a measure of self-acceptance and self-knowledge.

400. Woodward, A.G. "The Emergence of the Self: James Boswell in His Journals." English Studies in Africa: A Journal of the Humanities 19 (1976): 57-63.

Considers the self-consciousness of Boswell's journals representative of European civilization's development in the eighteenth century of "an outlook on life more attuned to variety, freedom and individualism than any which had hitherto existed."

401. Rogal, Samuel J. "Boswell's 'Scheme of Living': London on Six Shillings a Day." Research Studies 44 (1976): 126-36.

Provides a month-by-month inventory of Boswell's income and expenditures in London from November 1762 to August 1763.

402. Baker, Van R. "A French Provincial City and Three English Writers: Montpellier as Seen in the 1760s by Sterne, Smollett, and Boswell." Eighteenth-Century Life 2 (1976): 54-58.

Asserts that the observations of Sterne, Smollett, and Boswell provide "a glimpse into eighteenth-century urban life outside the capital." Excerpts comments from Boswell's journal on the weather, accommodations, architecture, wine, and people of Montpellier.

403. Reed, Joseph W. and Frederick A. Pottle, Introduction. Boswell: Laird of Auchinleck, 1778-1782. The Yale Editions of the Private Papers of James Boswell. Edited by Joseph W. Reed and Frederick A. Pottle. New York and London: McGraw-Hill, 1977. xi-xxxiv.

Explains that this volume ends with Boswell's inheritance of Auchinleck, its major theme a constellation of problems that continue to plague Boswell: the failing health of his wife, a troubled relationship with his father, struggles with alcohol and sexual temptation, a declining legal practice. Notes that Boswell, on the other hand, was buoyed by his literary reputation, his friendships with famous men, and a host of literary projects. Suggests that the power of this journal lies in its brilliant moments and memorable scenes, being "richer in developed instant and incident" than in plot.

404. Byrd, Max. "The Happy Valley and Its Discontents." London Transformed: Images of the City in the Eighteenth Century. New Haven: Yale University Press, 1978. 80-118.

Places Boswell's London Journal in the broader context of eighteenth-century literature that expresses "the city's chaotic effect upon human nature" and examines Boswell's "extraordinary relationship" with London: his tremendous love for the spectacle and variety of the city, his attraction to "the coarse, disheartening" underworld, his use of the city as a stage for his "theatrical debauchery," as "an arena in which to strive for fame, notice of any kind."

405. Nussbaum, Felicity A. "Father and Son in Boswell's London Journal." Philological Quarterly 57 (1978): 383-97.

Views the London Journal as "a metaphoric act of rebellion" against his dominating father: Boswell focuses on literary renderings of father-son conflict (Henry IV, Hamlet, the story of Joseph in Genesis); he pursues a military career and sexual pleasure in opposition to his father's advice; he self-consciously plays the role of father himself in writing about his illegitimate son, Charles; and he wins the esteem of the illustrious Samuel Johnson, "the antithesis" of his own father. Argues that the conclusion of the London Journal represents not so much Boswell's capitulation as his maturation: he receives permission to go into the Guards, though he chooses not to act on it, and, more importantly, he continues, despite his father's disapproval, to keep his journal, a symbol of his independence.

406. Kay, Donald. "Boswell in the Green-Room: Dramatic Method in the London Journal, 1762-1763." Philological Quarterly 57 (1978): 195-212.

Believes that Boswell in the London Journal blends the objectivity of biography and the subjectivity of autobiography and creates distance between Boswell the Author and Boswell the Hero by employing theatrical metaphors and techniques: he plays roles, conceiving of himself as literary heroes (Aeneus, Mr. Spectator) and as real-life models (Johnson, Digges); he renders particular scenes in the manner of a dramatist, using externals--dialogue, setting, costume, and props--to reveal inner feelings; and he structures the whole of the Louisa affair as a comedy of manners.

407. Steinke, Jim. "Boswell on the Grand Tour (Germany and Switzerland) 1764: Belle Epoque for the Man in Search of a Character." New Rambler: Journal of the Johnson Society of London 22 (1980): 29-40.

Locates as a source of unity in Boswell on the Grand Tour: Germany and Switzerland, 1764 Boswell's conception of himself as a young laird: unlike the London Journal, which dramatizes Boswell's anxious search for models and attempt to recreate himself, this volume reveals Boswell to be happy, confident, secure with the image of himself as a young aristocrat, Baron Boswell, like his traveling companion, Lord Marischal, a man of the world.

408. Frieman, Joy. "Artful Memory: The Journals of James Boswell." Dissertation, Rutgers University, 1980.

Studies the journals as an imaginative and candid life history, a record of his conflicts of identity, and a landmark in the development of autobiography. Pays particular attention to the history of first-person writing in England, Boswell's skill as an interviewer, and his reputation as a biographer and autobiographer.

409. Brady, Frank. "Boswell's London Journal: The Question of Memorial and Imaginative Modes." Literature and Society: The Lawrence Henry Gipson Symposium, 1978. Edited by Jan Fergus. Bethlehem, PA: Lawrence Gipson Institute, 1981. 33-47.

Classifies Boswell's London Journal as memorial, a work based on memory, and notes that the modern preference for imaginative works is a "historical development" rather than a "critical absolute." Argues that the tendency of modern critics to treat memorial works as imaginative--to analyze the London Journal as if it were a novel--is to overlook how readers actually respond to such works: readers bring a different set of expectations and assumptions to memorial and imaginative works. Argues that even though the London Journal displays coherence and its structure can be analyzed in novelistic terms, the questions of correspondence and content should not be ignored. Suggests that the London Journal is so appealing because the openness of the diary form corresponds to readers' experience of life, where endings are likewise unknown, and because Boswell combines a "normative sensibility" with exceptional expressive power.

410. Harris, Mark, ed. The Heart of Boswell: Six Journals in One Volume. New York: McGraw-Hill, 1981. VI-VII, 3-5, 69-70, 119-21, 163-65, 219-21, 311-14.

Introduces a distillation of the first six volumes of the Yale Editions of the Private Papers of James Boswell with a focus on Boswell's completion of those tasks he set for himself between 1762 and 1774: to meet Johnson, Rousseau, and Voltaire; to complete his studies; to tour Europe and visit Corsica; to pacify his father; to publish; to marry; and to defend John Reid.

411. Lustig, Irma S. Introduction. Boswell: The Applause of the Jury, 1782-1785. The Yale Editions of the Private Papers of James Boswell. Edited by Irma S. Lustig and Frederick A. Pottle. New York and London: McGraw-Hill, 1981. xi-xxv.

Explains that the journal of this period records a success--Boswell's devoted efforts to improve and manage his estate at Auchinleck--and a triumph--his preparation of Hebrides for publication. Notes that the journal also contains a full record of Boswell's metaphysical doubts, the last of Johnson's conversation, and material Boswell labeled "Tacenda"--anecdotes from Garrick and Elizabeth Desmoulins concerning Johnson's sexual potency and appetite--these transcripts displaying "all of the novelist's skills except fable."

412. Kay, Donald and Carol McGinnis Kay. "The Face in the Mirror of Boswell's London Journal." Bulletin of the Modern Language Society 83.2 (1982): 192-202.

Examines Boswell's self-presentation in the London Journal as he first imagines and then lives his life. Suggests that his constant role-playing not only gives the journal its distinctive shape; it also serves an important psychological function for the young and narcissistic Boswell: by observing the reactions of various audiences to his posing, Boswell attempts to bolster "an immature ego," to strengthen his "underdeveloped sense of self."

413. Kullman, Colby H. "Boswell's Account of the 'lesher of Hillend': A Total Plan for a Criminal Drama." Ball State University Forum 23.3 (1982): 25-34.

Analyzes Boswell's journal account of the last days and execution of the sheep stealer John Reid as a dramatic whole, complete with exposition, complications, ambiguous climax, and epilogue. Praises Boswell's skillful characterization, his handling of dramatic irony, and his ability to create, rather than play upon, emotion.

414. Gribble, Francis. "Boswell's Dutch Flirtation." The Nineteenth Century and After 72 (1912): 942-52.

Identifies Zélide, mentioned in Boswell's letters to Temple, as Belle Van Zuylen; provides a sketch of her life and traces her correspondence with Boswell.

415. Tinker, Chauncey B. "New Chapter of Boswell; Unpublished Letters to Rousseau and Voltaire." Atlantic Monthly 127 (1921): 577-83.

Prints Boswell's letter of introduction to Rousseau; summarizes Boswell's accounts of his interviews with Rousseau and Voltaire.

416. Tinker, Chauncey B. "Boswell's Letters to Rousseau." Literary Review 2 (1922): 703-4.

Prints four letters from Boswell to Rousseau discovered among Rousseau's papers in the Public Library of Neuchatel.

417. Canby, Henry S. "What Professor Tinker Cut." New Republic, 25 Mar. 1925: 127.

Defends Tinker's belief that several phrases in Boswell's letters are "unprintable."

418. Pottle, Frederick A. "Boswell's Miss W---t." Notes and Queries 148 (1925): 80.

Identifies the "Miss W---t" mentioned in Boswell's letter to Temple of 29 July 1758--"Extremely pretty, and posest of every amiable qualification"--as Martha White (or Whytt), who married the Earl of Elgin in 1759.

419. Whibley, Leonard. "Boswell Without Johnson." Blackwood's Magazine, Feb. 1925: 250-70.

Examines Boswell's letters to Temple as a record of his life and character, focusing on his legal career, quest for a wife, literary endeavors, ambition, and vanity.

420. Sherman, Stuart. "Boswell on His Own Hook." Critical Woodcuts. New York: Charles Scribner's Sons, 1926. 271-83.

Argues that Tinker's edition of the letters explodes once and for all the myth that Boswell is interesting solely in relation to Johnson and suggests that Boswell's genius lay not in hero worship, but in a passion for the richness of life, a passion that led him not only to Johnson but also to Rousseau, Voltaire, Paoli, and Wilkes.

The letters reveal that Boswell's friendship with Johnson and the writing of the Life made up only a part of a "many-sided, adventurous and ambitious career, full and running over with experience."

421. Simpson, T.B. "The Letters of Boswell." Fortnightly Review 127 (March 1927): 376-89.

Considers Boswell's greatness as a letter writer to be his ability to tell the truth about himself: especially in his best, most candid letters to Temple, he reveals his true nature, introspective and melancholy, manically energetic and high-spirited, unorthodox in love, admirable in friendship. Believes that Boswell, though writing in the roles of father, landlord, biographer, was always "conscious of an invisible audience"--posterity.

422. Pottle, Frederick A. "His Own Boswell." Saturday Review of Literature, 20 July 1929: 1187-88.

Reviews Boswell's correspondence with Zélide.

423. Inge, Charles C. "Two More Boswell Letters." Times Literary Supplement, 27 Mar. 1930: 274.

Describes unpublished letters from Boswell to Ralph Churchton.

424. Bennett, Charles H. "Letters Between the Honourable Andrew Erskine and James Boswell, Esq." Dissertation, Yale University, 1932.

This dissertation is not available from University Microfilms International and does not circulate.

425. Wecter, Dixon. "Four Unpublished Letters from Boswell to Burke." Modern Philology 36 (1938): 47-58.

Introduces and prints four letters to Burke found among the private papers of Burke at Wentworth Woodhouse, Yorkshire, the letters revealing Boswell's yearning for political preferment and his sincere admiration for Burke.

426. Wecter, Dixon. "Dr. Johnson, Mrs. Thrale and Boswell: Three Letters." Modern Language Notes 56 (1941): 525-29.

Prints a letter dated 30 August 1776 from Boswell to his uncle John Boswell, M.D., rejecting a request for money.

427. Chapman, R.W. "Johnson's Letters to Boswell." Review of English Studies 18 (1942): 323-28.

Notes that of Johnson's letters printed in the Life, only those to Boswell have not been discovered. Provides a table listing the date of each letter with a reference to the Life, and Boswell's record of receipt with a reference to the private papers.

428. Chapman, R.W. "The Johnson-Boswell Correspondence." Notes and Queries 185 (1943): 32-39.

Provides a chronology of the Boswell-Johnson correspondence, with cross-references to the Hill-Powell edition of the Life and to Boswell's private papers.

429. Chapman, R.W. "The Johnson-Boswell Correspondence." Notes and Queries 186 (1944): 45-47.

Makes additions and corrections to Item 428.

430. Chapman, R.W. "Johnson and Boswell." Times Literary Supplement, 2 Mar. 1946: 103.

Attempts to establish the chronology of Johnson's correspondence with Boswell in the summer of 1784.

431. "Unpublished Burke Papers." Times Literary Supplement, 30 Sept. 1949: 640.

Prints three letters from Boswell to Burke.

432. Weis, Charles, McC. "The Correspondence of James Boswell and Sir David Dalrymple." Dissertation, Yale University, 1952.

This dissertation is not available from University Microfilms International and does not circulate.

433. Dixon, Arthur W. "The Correspondence of James Boswell and His Sons, Alexander and James." Dissertation, Yale University, 1953.

This dissertation is not available from University Microfilms International and does not circulate.

434. Fifer, Charles N. "Editing Boswell: A Search for Letters." Manuscript 6 (1953): 2-5.

Explains that the most time-consuming task for an editor of Boswell's correspondence is the discovery of the letters themselves, many of which are part of the Yale collection, but hundreds more are either lost or owned by public libraries and museums and individual collectors.

435. Hoover, Andrew G. "Boswell's Letters at Newhailes." University of Toronto Quarterly 22 (1953): 244-60.

Prints and annotates the text of ten letters from Boswell to Dalrymple, and one from Dalrymple to Boswell, all discovered in 1937 in the library of Sir Mark Dalrymple at Newhailes.

436. Carnie, Robert H. "A Letter from Lord Hailes to James Boswell in Holland." Notes and Queries, n.s. 1 (1954): 63-65.

Prints a letter dated 27 June 1764 found among the Laing manuscripts of the University of Edinburgh, from Dalrymple to Boswell.

437. Roberts, S.C. "More Boswell Letters." Times Literary Supplement, 1 Jan. 1954: 16.

Reports the discovery of a packet of sixty letters from Boswell to his cousin Robert Boswell.

438. Burke, Mary D. "Selected Correspondences of James Boswell, 1770-1773." Dissertation, Yale University, 1955.

This dissertation is not available from University Microfilms International and does not circulate.

439. Cole, Richard C. "The Correspondence of James Boswell in 1769." Dissertation, Yale University, 1955.

This dissertation is not available from University Microfilms International and does not circulate.

440. Irving, William H. The Providence of Wit in the English Letter Writers. Durham, NC: Duke University Press, 1955. 300-306, et passim.

Contrasts the silly, sentimental, and artificial Letters Between the Honourable Andrew Erskine and James Boswell, Esq. with Boswell's genuinely witty and unaffected letters to Temple. Notes Boswell's ability to adapt himself to his correspondent and his wide range of tones--formal, forthright, flattering, naive.

441. Gray, James. "Boswell's Brother Confessor: William Johnson Temple." Tennessee Studies in Literature 4 (1959): 61-71.

Characterizes Boswell's lifelong correspondent Temple as "a protesting, but not unwilling confessor," a scholarly, shrewd, and tolerant friend who understood Boswell's complex character--puritanical and licentious, gay and melancholy, ambitious and self-destructive.

442. Hankins, Nellie Pottle. "The Correspondence of James Boswell and James Bruce." Dissertation, University of Kansas, 1960.

Includes one hundred letters, most appearing for the first time, between Boswell and James Bruce, first overseer of Auchinleck. These letters reveal Boswell in his role of laird and provide information about his father, wife, children, tenants, and eighteenth-century agriculture.

443. Houston, Benjamin F. "James Boswell." Notes and Queries, n.s. 10 (1963): 154.

Asks if the line "I am in love beyond the Salt Sea" (Boswell to Johnston, 21 September 1768) is from a song or ballad.

444. Hankins, John David. "Early Correspondence of James Boswell: 1757-1766." 2 vols. Dissertation, Indiana University, 1964.

Contains a selection of 154 letters to and from Boswell, the main correspondents being Andrew Erskine, Dempster, and Wilkes.

445. Isles, Duncan E. "Other Letters in the Lennox Collection." Times Literary Supplement, 5 Aug. 1965: 685.

Describes a letter from Boswell to Charlotte Lennox found in the collection among those by Richardson, Garrick, and Reynolds.

446. Reiberg, Rufus. "James Boswell's Personal Correspondence: The Dramatized Quest for Identity." The Familiar Letter in the Eighteenth Century. Edited by Howard Anderson, Philip B. Daghlian, and Irvin Ehrenpreis. Lawrence: University of Kansas Press, 1966. 244-68.

Characterizes Boswell's correspondence as essentially dramatic: playing the roles of actor, stage manager, and critic, Boswell attempts to establish his identity as a Great Man. Divides the letters into three types: first, the conventional social letters that keep friends and family informed of his activities; second, the contrived or artificial letters, essays cast in the form of letters, vehicles for wit best exemplified by Boswell's Shandean letters to Andrew Erskine; and third, the spontaneous, organically shaped letters, which, like the most memorable portions of the journal, dramatically portray his shifting states of consciousness.

447. Walker, Ralph S. Introduction. The Correspondence of James Boswell and John Johnston of Grange. Edited by Ralph S. Walker. The Yale Editions of the Private Papers of James Boswell. Research Edition Correspondence Vol. 1. New York: McGraw-Hill, 1966.

Suggests that the interest of this correspondence is neither narrative nor intellectual; rather it is the record "of a remarkable friendship." In his letters to Johnston, we see "Boswell at his best": affectionate, unreserved, and, above all, loyal. Johnston may have heightened young Boswell's enthusiasm for Jacobitism, Catholicism, romance, and revolt; later he served him as a sympathetic listener, a good companion, and a "steadying influence" whose death in 1786 left Boswell disturbingly separated from "the past, the traditional, the unchanging."

448. Clifford, James L. "Boswell, Johnson, and Their Friends." Columbia Library Columns 24.1 (1974): 10-20.

Describes previously unpublished letters of the Johnson Circle now in the possession of Columbia University. Gives the text of a letter from Boswell to George Colman, and excerpts of letters to Johnson from Piozzi, Elizabeth Montagu, and Anne Welch.

449. Fifer, Charles N. Introduction. The Correspondence of James Boswell with Certain Members of the Club, Including Oliver Goldsmith, Bishops Percy and Barnard, Sir Joshua Reynolds, Topham Beauclerk, and Bennet Langton. The Yale Editions of the Private Papers of James Boswell, Research Edition. Correspondence, Vol. 3. Edited by Charles N. Fifer. London: Heineman; New York: McGraw-Hill, 1976. xxi-xcix.

Notes that this edition of Boswell's correspondence with twenty-four members of The Club testifies to "the abiding attractiveness of his personality," reveals the full range of his interests--law, politics, literature--and sheds light on the problems he faced in the composition of Hebrides and especially the Life--gathering information, organizing his materials, polishing the text. Includes biographies of the correspondents, brief sketches for most, longer essays for Barnard, Beauclerk, Langton, and Percy.

450. Murphy, Victoria Thompson. "The Miscellaneous Correspondence of James Boswell, 1774-75." Dissertation, City University of New York, 1981.

Contains 115 letters, annotations, and an introduction.

451. Redford, Bruce B. "Correspondence of James Boswell, 1778-80." Dissertation, Princeton University, 1981.

This dissertation is not available from University Microfilms International and does not circulate.

452. Redford, Bruce B. "Boswell as Correspondent; Boswell as Letter-Writer." Yale University Library Gazette 56 (1982): 40-52.

Distinguishes between Boswell as correspondent, whose letters are important documents, valuable primary sources for the study of eighteenth-century Great Britain, and Boswell as letter writer, a literary craftsman, a shaper of individual texts, an artist in a well-established genre. Describes the appeal and significance of Boswell's correspondence: his range of acquaintanceships is fascinating, from farmers and criminals to lords and gentlemen, "a gallery of eighteenth-century people, unmasked, speaking in their own voices"; it is an anthology of eighteenth-century anecdote, news, politics, and social history; it reveals Boswell playing a great variety of roles--traveler, husband, laird, neighbor, biographer--and it allows a reader to balance his public and private selves: we understand not just the moody, dissolute Boswell of the journals, but the social, charming Boswell, "the nature and force of Boswell's impact on his extensive acquaintance." Evaluates Boswell as a letter writer and concludes that he ought not be included among the eighteenth-century masters of the genre: although he wrote outstanding individual letters, his epistolary oeuvre lacks quantity and versatility; he paid insufficient attention to the minutiae of familiar letters, for example, how to create rather than simply assume interest; his transparent style is too limited for the genre, his naive and earnest tone too monotonous; most important, he is unable or unwilling to tailor his letters for a particular audience, "to calculate rhetorical effects according to the identity of a given correspondent."

453. Crawford, Thomas. "Boswell's Temple and the Jane Austen World." Scottish Literary Journal: A Review of Studies in Scottish Literature and Language 10.2 (1983): 53-67.

Examines the Boswell-Temple correspondence and finds in Temple's account of his courtship, marriage, and family life the same emotions, predicaments, and social relationships that Jane Austen depicts in her novels.

454. Redford, Bruce B. "Boswell's 'Libertine' Correspondences." Philological Quarterly 63 (1984): 55-73.

Examines Boswell's correspondence with Henry Herbert, tenth Earl of Pembroke, and with Wilkes, both charming, witty rakes. Identifies superficial similarities in the correspondences--a spirited tone, a focus on women, politics, and literature--as well as fundamental differences. Notes that Boswell and Pembroke never achieved true friendship: Boswell's desire to compete, his attempts to conceal a sense of social inferiority, his hopes of winning a patron--these fix the correspondence in a series of formal gestures. Shows that Boswell and Wilkes, on the other hand, build on their idyllic time together in Italy, engage in an affectionate war of wits, and reveal a genuine friendship; at their best, they "create a solitary world of value" and "forge a bond of cultural and personal solidarity" in letters that are "worldly, mocking, and affectionate in turn, spirited, spontaneous, inflected by the cadences of the speaking voice."

455. Brown, J.T.T. "James Boswell as Essayist." Scotch Historical Review 18 (1921): 102-16.

Calls attention to the documentary rather than literary value of The Hypochondriack, treating it as a source of material for the study of Boswell and the Life. Believes that Boswell's purpose in writing essays was to prepare himself to write Johnson's biography and points out parallel discussions of topics such as diaries, conversation, and hypochondria in the Life and essays.

456. Bailey, Margery. "Boswell as Essayist." Journal of English and Germanic Philology 22 (1923): 412-23.

Praises Boswell's The Hypochondriack as "ingenius and charming." Notes that Boswell must have reviewed the essays in composing the Life, though challenges the notion that Boswell wrote them simply as a way to prepare himself for the writing of the Life: numerous references and parallels to Voltaire, Rousseau, and his own commonplace books and letters indicate his wide-ranging interests beyond Johnson. Conjectures that Boswell left off publishing the essays abruptly in 1783 not because he needed to devote himself more fully to collecting material on Johnson, but because of an "internal upheaval" at the London Magazine.

457. Pottle, Frederick A. "Boswelliana: Two Attributions." Notes and Queries 147 (1924): 281, 375.

Attributes two anonymous works to Boswell: Observations, Good or Bad, Stupid or Clever, Serious or Jocular, on Squire Foote's Dramatic Entertainment Intitled, THE MINOR. By a Genius and A View of the Edinburgh Theatre During the Summer Season, 1759, both published in 1760.

458. Pottle, Frederick A. "Boswell's 'Matrimonial Thought.' " Notes and Queries 147 (1924): 283.

Provides information about Boswell's "Matrimonial Thought," a poem published in The London Chronicle and copied into the Leeds Intelligencer in 1768. Identifies the "M.H." to whom the poem is addressed as Matthew Henderson, a gentleman of Ayrshire and Edinburgh and a friend of Burns.

459. Pottle, Frederick A. "Boswell's 'Observations on The Minor.' " Bulletin of the New York Public Library 29 (1925): 3-6.

Identifies Boswell as the author of Observations, Good or Bad, Stupid or Clever, Serious or Jocular, on Squire Foote's Dramatic Entertainment, Intitled THE MINOR. By a Genius, a

Shandean commentary on Samuel Foote's farce, published in Edinburgh in 1760, most likely at Boswell's own expense.

460. Pottle, Frederick A. "The Incredible Boswell." Blackwood's Magazine, Aug. 1925: 149-65.

Based on Boswell's own file of The London Chronicle, describes his contributions to that newspaper from 1767 to 1775: Boswell wrote roughly one hundred pieces, from single paragraphs to full essays, many of them devoted to Corsica and the Douglas Cause, some factual, but most invented--letters from fictional English soldiers in Corsica, adventures of a mysterious Corsican courier, glowing anonymous reviews of his own Dorando: A Spanish Tale.

461. Bailey, Margery. Introduction. The Hypochondriack: Being the Seventy Essays by the Celebrated Biographer, James Boswell, Appearing in the London Magazine from November, 1777 to August, 1783 and Here First Reprinted. 2 vols. Edited by Margery Bailey. Stanford: Stanford University Press, 1928. 3-99.

Rejects the notion that Boswell wrote these essays simply to shine as an author or to prepare himself for the writing of the Life or to justify his own behavior; suggests instead that their composition was a part of his lifelong attempt to make himself a good man--their chief purpose was mental and moral discipline. Boswell writes about topics such as the dangers of drunkenness and the superiority of pleasures of the mind to those of the senses not as a hypocrite, but as "a man in search of virtuous standards": he endorses virtuous principles, though opposed to his own habits, and sets forth his own defects honestly, though covertly, as examples to be avoided. Traces Boswell's debts to earlier writers, from classical allusions to unacknowledged borrowings from Montaigne, Addison, and Johnson, noting Boswell's increasing stylistic sophistication as he wrote the series. Concludes by placing the essays in the context of the literature of melancholy and by considering Boswell himself as a sufferer of the English Malady.

462. McKinlay, Robert. "Boswell's Fugitive Pieces." Records of the Glasgow Bibliographical Society 8 (1930): 64-77.

Provides a chronological survey and bibliography of Boswell's fugitive pieces, from the Ode to Tragedy (1761) to No Abolition of Slavery, or the Universal Empire of Love (1791).

463. Bailey, Margery. "James Boswell: Lawyer or Press Agent?" Dalhousie Review 10 (1931): 481-94.

Characterizes Boswell's activities in the Douglas Cause as those of a press agent: through the publication of his Dorando: A Spanish Tale and a series of advertisements, reviews, pamphlets, letters, and verses, he sought to create public support for the Douglas side, proving himself an effective manipulator of opinion if not a great respecter of legal processes.

464. Foster, Finley. "Piozzian Rhymes." Times Literary Supplement, 30 Mar. 1933: 230.

Provides further evidence of Boswell's authorship of "Piozzian Rhymes," published in The London Chronicle, 18-20 April 1786.

465. Murray, John. "Boswell and 'The Scots Magazine.' " The Scots Magazine, n.s. 33 (1940): 275-82.

Lists and describes Boswell's contributions to The Scots Magazine: between 1758 and 1786 he published verses, commentary on the Douglas Cause, reports--genuine and fabricated--from Corsica, an account of the Shakespeare Jubilee at Stratford, and two political letters to the people of Scotland.

466. Murray, John. "Notes on Johnson's Movements in Scotland. Suggested Attributions to Boswell in the Caledonian Mercury." Notes and Queries 178 (1940): 3-5, 182-85.

Attributes to Boswell a number of articles--on Johnson's tour of Scotland, Boswell's court cases, Lady MacDonald's masquerade--that appeared in the Caledonian Mercury, 1773-74.

467. Thompson, Karl F. "An Anonymous 'Epistle to James Boswell.' " Notes and Queries 194 (1949): 162-63.

Speculates that Boswell may be the author of the anonymous "Epistle to James Boswell," a verse satire published in the Gentleman's Magazine for June 1787.

468. Pottle, Frederick A. Introduction. James Boswell, Andrew Erskine, and George Dempster, Critical Strictures on the New Tragedy of Elvira Written by Mr. David Malloch (1763). Los Angeles: William Andrews Clark Memorial Library, University of California, 1952. i-vii.

Explains that Boswell, Andrew Erskine, and Dempster decided to damn Elvira well in advance of attending the play on 19 January 1763, their hostility to Malloch, a fellow Scotsman, the result of his repudiating his country: he had changed his name and disguised his humble origins as the son of a tenant farmer. Admits that the piece is the "merest of trifles," a useful footnote to the London Journal and of some interest to students of eighteenth-century British drama.

469. Chapman, R.W. "Boswell Without Johnson." Johnsonian and Other Essays and Reviews. London: Oxford University Press, 1953. 182-86.

Reviews Margery Bailey's edition of The Hypochondriack, calling the essays "surprisingly good," and predicting that their publication would enhance Boswell's literary reputation.

470. Carnie, Robert H. "Boswell's Projected History of Ayrshire." Notes and Queries, n.s. 2 (1955): 250-51.

Points out references to Boswell's projected history of Ayrshire county in his journals and correspondence, and in the correspondence of the antiquarians George Paton and Richard Gough.

471. Cole, Richard C. "James Boswell and the Irish Press, 1767-1795." Bulletin of the New York Public Library 73 (1969): 581-98.

Surveys Boswell's writing and responses to it published in Irish newspapers and magazines. Describes announcements, reviews, and extracts of his works as well as descriptions of his activities on behalf of the Corsicans and of his travels with Johnson. Concludes that Boswell's reputation in Ireland was that of a major literary figure.

472. Cole, Richard C. "A New Letter by James Boswell." Studies in Scottish Literature 8 (1970): 118-22.

Attributes to Boswell a pseudonymous letter published in a Dublin newspaper in 1769 requesting aid for Corsica.

473. McFarland, Ronald E. " 'No Abolition of Slavery': Boswell and the Slave Trade." New Rambler: Journal of the Johnson Society of London 112 (1972): 55-64.

Examines Boswell's poetic contribution to the debate surrounding the proposed abolition of the slave trade in 1791, "No Abolition of Slavery; or the Universal Empire of Love." Notes that although the arguments may strike a twentieth-century reader as reactionary or inhumane, Boswell's sentiments reflect both his lifelong devotion to the principle of subordination and the widely held belief that slavery is a natural condition and in the best interests of those enslaved.

474. Lustig, Irma S. "The Manuscript as Biography: Boswell's Letter to the People of Scotland 1785." Papers of the Bibliographical Society of America 68 (1974): 237-50.

Argues that Boswell's extensive revisions in the manuscript of his second Letter to the People of Scotland show that he was troubled by two questions: how harshly to treat his political opponents and how much information about himself to include. The final version, which includes both attacks on Dundas and Fergusson and numerous autobiographical asides, ought to be considered the product not, as one critic has suggested, of drunkenness, but of "agitated choices."

475. Werner, Jack. Introduction. Boswell's Book of Bad Verse (A Verse Self-Portrait), or, Love Poems and Other Verses. Edited by Jack Werner. London: White Lion, 1974.

Describes this collection of seventy-one verses, written between 1758 and 1762, most of which are published here for the first time. Characterizes Boswell as an extremely limited poet, but finds in the verses "a fascinating mosaic portrait of the man."

476. Tarbert, David M. Introduction. A View of the Edinburgh Theatre During the Summer Season, 1759. The Augustan Reprint Society Publication no. 179. Los Angeles: Clark Memorial Library, 1976.

Examines the View as Boswell's first public exploration of ideas concerning acting and the theater: the superiority of natural over artificial acting styles, the relationship between acting and masquerade, and the psychological dangers of acting, especially a multiple consciousness that "threatens the unity and identity of the self."

477. Mace-Tessler, Eric. "The Development of the Eighteenth-Century English Periodical Essay." Dissertation, Boston University Graduate School, 1981.

Considers Boswell's The Hypochondriack in light of the development of the periodical essay form toward greater freedom and complexity.

GENERAL STUDIES

477a. Fitzgerald, Percy. "Some Bozzyana." The Gentleman's Magazine (Feb. 1902): 191-203.

Calls attention to items of interest from Boswell's library, mainly his critical opinions written on the fly-leaves, and prints eight letters from Boswell to Wilkes.

478. Bergengren, R. "Boswell's Chapbooks and Others." Lamp 28 (Feb. 1904): 39-44.

Calls attention to a collection of chapbooks, now at Harvard, bound by Boswell under the title "Curious Productions" with a note describing the pleasure he took in such books as a boy and stating his desire to write his own "little story book."

479. Bicknell, Percy F. "A Prince of Interviewers." Dial, 1 March 1905: 141-44.

Challenges Macaulay's claim that Boswell was "one of the smallest men who ever lived" and argues that he was not only a great biographer but also a great interviewer--insatiably curious and doggedly accurate.

480. Caldwell, Joshua W. "A Brief for Boswell." Sewanee Review 13 (1905): 336-51.

Defends Boswell from charges that he was a silly, dissolute sychophant by suggesting that he was not so immoral as Byron or Shelley and by arguing that the Life is undeniable evidence of his intelligence, judgment, and literary genius.

481. "Boswell." Blackwood's Magazine, Feb. 1909: 233-51.

Challenges Macaulay's harsh judgment of Boswell's character and while admitting Boswell's weaknesses for women and alcohol, enumerates his attractive qualities--honesty, generosity, genius for friendship. Describes Johnson as Boswell's "hero" and also his "vocation."

482. Richardson, J.J. "Bozzy." Manchester Quarterly 28 (1909): 234-45.

Surveys Boswell's career, finding in the unhappiness of his later life the "penalty" for youthful "indulgence and recklessness." Reaffirms Macaulay's judgment of the Life but not of its author: though undoubtedly weak, eccentric, possibly mad, Boswell possessed "exceptional powers of feeling, of observation, and of sympathy."

483. Mallory, George. Boswell the Biographer. London: Smith Elder, 1912.

Surveys Boswell's life and character and assesses his biographical achievement: Boswell combines a scientist's devotion to objective truth and an artist's understanding of human nature and drama. Believes that Hebrides and especially the Life represent a triumph of on-the-spot reporting: "It seems to have been his common habit to sit down, note-book in hand, to record conversation." Suggests that Boswell's portrayal of Johnson, though more "awful" and less playful than the Johnson memorialized by Fanny Burney and others, is nevertheless true not only to his own impressions but also to real aspects of Johnson's character.

484. Cosulich, Gilbert. "Johnson's Affection for Boswell." Sewanee Review 22 (1914): 151-55.

Suggests that Johnson "felt something akin to parental affection" for Boswell, noting that Johnson frequently praised Boswell's abilities and professed his own sincere attachment to him.

485. Walker, Hugh. "Wise Men Who Have Passed for Fools." Yale Review 5 (1916): 587-604.

Considers Steele, Goldsmith, and Boswell gifted writers with unjustified reputations as foolish men. Believes that Boswell's self-conscious artistry in the Life and Johnson's esteem for him prove that he was not the fool Macaulay portrayed him to be but rather a man of powerful understanding and remarkable wisdom.

486. Barker, F.W.E. "Boswell's Record of Johnson's Table-Talk." Papers of the Manchester Literary Club 43 (1917): 93-114.

Recounts Boswell's meeting with Johnson and praises Boswell for his diligence and dramatic instinct.

487. Morley, Christopher. "Two Days We Celebrate." Mince Pie: Adventures on the Sunny Side of Grub Street. New York: Doran, 1919. 117-31.

Celebrates Johnson's meeting Boswell, an eighteenth-century Pepys, "a droll, vain, erring, bibulous, warm-hearted creature," but above all, a great diarist.

488. "When Boswell Dared to Differ." Times Literary Supplement, 9 Jan. 1919: 13-14.

Reviews areas of disagreement between Boswell and Johnson.

489. Brown, J.T.T. "James Boswell: An Episode of His Grand Tour (1763-1766)." Transactions of the Glasgow Archeaological Society, n.s. 7 (1920): 197-215.

Prints a long letter from Boswell to Zélide, written from Berlin and dated 9 July 1764, and suggests that Boswell would have married her had her father consented to the match.

490. Barfield, Owen. "Boswell." New Statesman, 13 Aug. 1921: 520.

Considers Boswell's "cheerful folly" his most endearing trait.

491. Lucas, St. John. "Vagabond Impressions: Rousseau and Boswell." Blackwood's Magazine, Nov. 1922: 631-38.

Describes the circumstances of the meeting between Rousseau and Boswell, "one of the tragic and one of the most comic figures in eighteenth-century literature."

492. Roth, Georges. "James Boswell and Jean-Jacques Rousseau." London Mercury, Sept. 1923: 493-506.

Prints Boswell's letter of introduction to Rousseau as well as later correspondence discussing Voltaire, his travels, and Corsica. Includes comments on Boswell made by Hume and Deleyre in letters to Rousseau and speculates as to the cause of the estrangement between Boswell and Rousseau.

493. Whibley, Leonard. "Boswell's Journals." Blackwood's Magazine, Mar. 1923: 395-406.

Describes Boswell's lifelong habit of keeping a journal, expresses regret that the journals themselves seem to have been lost, and suggests that the virtues of a good journalist--candor, humor, a clear style, an eye for detail--are responsible for the unique excellence of the Life.

494. Murdock, Harold. Earl Percy Dines Abroad, a Boswellian Episode. Boston: Houghton Mifflin Co., 1924.

Provides a fictionalized account of a dinner given in 1778 by Paoli in honor of Earl Percy.

495. Pottle, Frederick A. " 'A North Briton Extraordinary.' " Notes and Queries 147 (1924): 259-61, 403, 404.

Questions the authorship of two pamphlets, both entitled A North Briton Extraordinary, published in 1765 and 1769 and sometimes attributed to Boswell. Suggests that Boswell is not the author.

496. Drinkwater, John. "Johnson and Boswell." The Muse in Council. London: Sidwick and Jackson, 1925. 218-24.

Argues that Boswell, though he vividly captures the sociable, "clubable" Johnson, fails to portray an essential side of his character: the lonely artist, "living apart through a great deal of his time in meditation, his mind discovering itself almost in secrecy."

497. "The Greatest of All Biographers." Current Opinion, Apr. 1925: 429-32.

Argues that new editions of Boswell's Corsica and Hebrides and Tinker's edition of the letters reveal Boswell to be a fascinating figure in his own right.

498. Pottle, Frederick A. "Boswellian Myths." Notes and Queries 149 (1925): 4-6, 21-22, 41-42.

Examines the evidence for and finally dismisses as false four stories about Boswell: that he made a tour with Margaret Caroline Rudd, that he accompanied the convicted murderer James Hackman in the mourning coach to Tyburn, that he compiled and published a summary of speeches and arguments in the Douglas Cause, and that he is the author of "A Poetical Address in Favour of the Corsicans."

499. Pottle, Frederick A. "Boswellian Notes." Notes and Queries 149 (1925): 113-14, 131-32, 184-86, 222.

Attributes to Boswell a pamphlet entitled "Reflections on the Late Alarming Bankruptcies in Scotland" (1772) and notes that Boswell's "Verses in the Character of a Corsican, at Shakespeare's Jubilee" were published not only in newspapers and magazines but also separately, probably as a broadside for distribution at the Shakespeare Jubilee in Stratford. Suggests that Boswell is the editor of Letters of Lady Jane Douglas (1767) and the author of the prefatory materials and notes. Describes three pirated editions of Boswell's Corsica published in Ireland.

500. Pottle, Frederick A. "Bozzy and Yorick." Blackwood's Magazine, Mar. 1925: 297-313.

Establishes that Boswell and Sterne met in the spring of 1760 by attributing to Boswell "An Original Letter, From a Gentleman of Scotland to the Earl of *** in London," in which Sterne is described as "the best companion I ever knew." Calls attention to an unpublished poetic epistle to Sterne that indicates Sterne heard and praised Boswell's Shandean poem, "The Cub at Newmarket."

501. Pottle, Frederick A. "The Part Played by Horace Walpole and James Boswell in the Quarrel Between Rousseau and Hume." Philological Quarterly 4 (1925): 351-63. Reprint. Horace Walpole: Writer, Politician, and Connoisseur. Essays on the 250th Anniversary of Walpole's Birth. Edited by Warren H. Smith. New Haven: Yale University Press, 1967. 255-291.

Prints several letters, possibly by Boswell, defending Rousseau and attacking Walpole. Includes also Boswell's verse in the character of Rousseau, originally published anonymously in The London Chronicle.

502. Sergeant, Philip W. Liars and Fakers. London: Hutchinson, 1925. 254-55.

Describes Boswell's connection with the literary forger W.H. Ireland: Boswell visited his exhibition of Shakespeariana and thought it genuine.

503. Wilson, Edmund. "Boswell and Others." New Republic 43 (July 1925): 153-54.

Distinguishes between the enjoyment of Boswell's Johnson and a genuine interest in literature, arguing that Boswell, "though he does to be sure write the most entertaining of literary day-books," has little intellectual or artistic importance.

504. Merritt, E. Percival. "Piozzi on Boswell and Johnson." Harvard Library Notes 2 (Apr. 1926): 104-11.

Describes and reconstructs the histories of a copy of the eighth edition of the Life and a copy of the second edition of the Hebrides, both owned and annotated by Piozzi and acquired by Harvard Library.

505. Skrine, Francis Henry, ed. "The Johnson Circle: Goldsmith, Dr. Percy, Boswell, Dr. Taylor, Tom Davies, Mrs. Williams, Frank Barber." Gossip About Dr. Johnson and Others, Being Chapters from the Memoirs of Laetitia M. Hawkins. London: Eveleigh, Nash and Grayson, 1926. 123-36.

Contains Laetitia Hawkins's remembrances of Boswell, emphasizing his vanity and social presumption but admitting the superiority of his Life over her father's "cold, stiff, and turgid" biography.

506. Lynd, Robert. "Boswell." Dr. Johnson and Company. London: Hodder, 1927; New York: Doubleday, 1928. 43-82.

Considers Boswell a man of "extraordinary original genius" but finally inseparable from Johnson in our imaginations. Notes Boswell's gift for comedy and self-dramatization, his contradictory urges toward morality and debauchery, his willingness to behave ridiculously in order to provoke Johnson to speak memorably. Suggests that the liberties Boswell took in reporting Johnson's conversation in the Life are artistically justified: they effectively convey the essential truth of Johnson's character.

507. MacPhail, J.R. "James Boswell, Esq." Cornhill Magazine 63 (July 1927): 31-43.

Suggests that Boswell's character was essentially that of a child: he possessed "an eager and catholic curiosity" and displayed a tremendous capacity for delight and admiration but lacked a serious moral sense: "Life was not a problem in conduct to him: it was a game to be played, and he played it in the way he liked best."

508. Pottle, Frederick A. "Portraits of James Boswell." Notes and Queries 152 (1927): 80-81.

Requests information concerning portraits by Nathaniel Hone, Henry Singleton, Sir Thomas Lawrence, and Raeburn, and sketches by George Langton and Samuel Wale.

509. Windle, Bertram C.A. "Bozzy." Catholic World 125 (1927): 433-42.

Speculates that if not for Boswell, Johnson would not be considered the greatest figure of his age, concluding that "Boswell made Johnson." Praises Boswell's good humor and summarizes his conversations with Johnson on the topic of Catholicism.

510. "Boswell and His Father." Blackwood's Magazine, Mar. 1928: 325-42.

Sketches the life and character of Alexander Boswell--his integrity and inflexible principles, his passion for Auchinleck and the classics, his antipathy toward Johnson--and traces his tumultuous relationship with James, whose character was "the antithesis" of his own.

511. Pleadwell, Frank L. "Lord Mountstuart--Boswell's Maecenas." American Collector 5 (1928): 233-41.

Prints five letters from Lord Mountstuart to William Hamilton written around the time Mountstuart and Boswell were together in Italy. The letters make no reference to Boswell.

512. Dunn, Waldo H. "Jamie Boswell's Thorn in the Flesh." South Atlantic Quarterly 28 (1929): 71-82.

Summarizes the career of Peter Pindar (John Walcot) and praises for their cleverness his satires aimed at Johnson's biographers, "Poetical and Congratulatory Epistle to James Boswell, Esquire" and "Bozzy and Piozzi."

513. Macphail, Andrew. "Johnson's Life of Boswell." Quarterly Review 253 (1929): 42-73.

Constructs from Johnson's letters an account of Boswell's life and vindication of his character, emphasizing Johnson's esteem and affection for Boswell, and suggesting that the harshest critics of Boswell--Macaulay and Carlyle--misinterpret his "amiable facetiousness," mistakenly assuming that Boswell is not very well aware of his sometimes comic self-presentation.

514. Parsons, Mrs. Clement. "Boswell's Tact." Life and Letters 3 (Dec. 1929): 503-13.

Attributes Boswell's success in courting great men to "a core of sympathetic sagacity."

515. Birrell, Augustine. "Boswell Disrobed!" Et Cetera. London: Chatto and Windus, 1930. 13-45.

Considers the posthumous publication of Boswell's private papers the suitable culmination of a process of public undressing--literary self-revelation--begun in his published letters, Corsica, Hebrides, and Life.

516. Ashmun, Margaret. The Singing Swan: An Account of Anna Seward and Her Acquaintance with Dr. Johnson, Boswell and Others of Their Time. New Haven: Yale University Press; London: Oxford University Press, 1931.

Examines Boswell's relationship with Anna Seward in light of her animosity toward Johnson: records Boswell's requests for information concerning Johnson, his ultimate rejection of the material he received, and his quarrel with her in 1793-94 in the Gentleman's Magazine over Johnson's character.

517. Gallaway, W.F. "Boswell and Sterne." Letters 5 (1931): 21-25, 30.

Examines Boswell's unpublished verse epistle to Sterne and speculates that Boswell may have met him in London in 1760. Suggests that Sterne, like Wilkes, appealed to Boswell because of his notoriety, his scandalous reputation; an acquaintance with Sterne represented still another way to defy the values of his father.

518. Cox, James E. "The Independent Boswell and the Capricious Dr. Johnson." Quarterly Journal, University of North Dakota 22 (1932): 51-59.

Argues that in judgments of particular works--especially those of Swift, Fielding, and Gray--Boswell, who was free of Johnson's personal prejudices, didacticism, and "extreme classicism," was the superior critic.

519. MacCarthy, Desmond. "Boswell." Criticism. New York: G.P. Putnam's Sons, 1932. 30-35.

Characterizes Boswell as he is revealed in his private papers as "the transparently honest man" and interprets his hypochondria as an acute self-consciousness, relieved only by drinking, sociability, and the companionship of great men.

520. Pearson, Hesketh. "Boswell as Artist." Cornhill Magazine 146 (1932): 704-11.

Regards Boswell as "a great creative artist" and Johnson as his dramatic creation. Notes that Boswell, though he gives an impression of absolute honesty, selects, distorts, and sometimes suppresses material to soften Johnson's faults and to reinforce his own image of him as a lovable eccentric.

521. Naughton, A.E.A. "James Boswell with Rousseau in 1764." Modern Language Forum 18 (1933): 47-54.

Describes Boswell's interviews with Rousseau and prints Boswell's record of their conversations.

522. Warnock, Robert. "Boswell and Wilkes in Italy." Journal of English Literary History 3 (1936): 257-69.

Summarizes and expands Boswell's notes on his meeting with Wilkes in Rome and Naples in 1765 and provides a record of their conversations on politics, literature, and women.

523. Bennett, Charles H. "The Auchinleck Entail." Times Literary Supplement, 27 Feb. 1937: 151.

Draws on Boswell's journal to explain his objection to his father's plan to entail the estate of Auchinleck upon heirs general.

524. Bingham, Sylvester H. "Publishing in the Eighteenth Century, with Special Reference to the Firm of Edward and Charles Dilly." Dissertation, Yale University, 1937.

This dissertation is not available from University Microfilms International and does not circulate.

525. Esdaile, K.A. "A Footnote to Boswell." Times Literary Supplement, 23 Oct. 1937: 783.

Prints the full text of Edward Dilly's epitaph and Boswell's account of his last interview with him.

526. McGuffie, Helen Louise. "The Personality of James Boswell." University of Pittsburgh Bulletin, Oct. 1937: 417-18.

Abstracts a master's thesis arguing that Boswell's ruling passion was a "desire to probe the recesses of his own soul, to know all sorts and conditions of men, and to taste each possible experience."

527. Boys, Richard C. "Boswell on Spelling." Modern Language Notes (1938): 600.

Calls attention to Boswell's orthographical practices as he outlines them in the Preface to his Corsica: he retains 'k' after 'c' and 'u' in 'our' endings.

528. Chapman, R.W. "The Hill-Powell Boswell." Times Literary Supplement, 31 Dec. 1938: 827.

Reports progress on the revision of Hill's edition of the Life and Hebrides.

529. Lincoln, Eleanor T. "James Boswell, Reader and Critic." Dissertation, Yale University, 1938.

Describes Boswell's knowledge of books, his habits of reading, and his literary taste.

530. Bryant, Donald C. "James Boswell." Edmund Burke and His Literary Friends. Washington University Studies in Language and Literature 9. St. Louis, 1939. 99-135.

Details, meeting by meeting and letter by letter, Boswell's "friendly intimacy" with Burke: his respect of Burke's abilities; his desire to become not just an acquaintance but an intimate friend; his recording of Burke's conversations; his requests for preferment. Suggests that Burke took Boswell "more casually than seriously, seldom seeking his company, but usually appearing to enjoy it."

531. Gaselee, Stephen. "Boswell to Reynolds, 1775." Notes and Queries 176 (1939): 427.

Replies to Item 532, explaining the Latin inscription on Gavin Hamilton's painting

532. N., S. "Boswell to Reynolds, 1775." Notes and Queries 176 (1939): 390, 427.

Seeks information regarding Gavin Hamilton's painting of Mary Queen of Scots done for Boswell.

533. Sewall, Richard B. "Rousseau's Second Discourse in England and Scotland from 1762 to 1772." Philological Quarterly 18 (1939): 225-42, esp. 230-37.

Studies the reception of Rousseau's Discourse on Inequality by several English and Scottish readers, including Boswell, who, as a young man, shared Rousseau's enthusiasm for liberty and the state of nature.

534. Belloc, Hilaire. "Boswell." Silence of the Sea, and Other Essays. London: Sheed and Ward, Inc., 1940. 71-75.

Believes that Boswell--perhaps the real hero of the Life--is humbly absorbed by a "fundamental human need--worship" and describes his prose as remarkably non-literary: he writes as unselfconsciously as one thinks.

535. "Boswell and His Ego: Some Bicentenary Reflections; A Reputation Redressed." Times Literary Supplement, 26 Oct. 1940: 542, 545.

Reviews the career of Boswell, among "the first rank of the world's diarists."

536. Keith, Alexander. "Boswell's Boswell." Listener 24 (7 Nov. 1940): 667-68.

Commemorates the two-hundredth anniversary of Boswell's birth by describing the Boswell that emerges from his own writing: not only a matchless biographer but also a resolute, courageous, admirably candid, and irrepressible man.

537. Warnock, Robert. "Boswell and Some Italian Literati." Interchange Fortnightly I (1940): 82-83.

Describes Boswell's meetings with Melchior Cesarotti and Giuseppe Baretti in Venice in 1765.

538. Warnock, Robert. "Boswell and Andrew Lumisden." Modern Language Quarterly 2 (1941): 601-7.

Describes Boswell's friendship with Lumisden, secretary to the Old Pretender, in Rome during 1765, including their "Horace Jaunt," a pilgrimage to the shrines of Horace.

539. Wimsatt, W.K., Jr. "Foote and a Friend of Boswell's: A Note on The Nabob." Modern Language Notes 57 (May 1942): 325-35.

Surveys the career of George Gray, Jr., a minor nabob and schoolfellow of Boswell's who may have served as a model for Sir Matthew Mitre, the hero of Foote's The Nabob.

540. Bronson, Bertrand H. "Boswell's Boswell." Johnson and Boswell, Three Essays. University of California Publications in English, 3.9: 399-429; Berkeley and Los Angeles: University of California Press, 1944. Reprint. Johnson Agonistes and Other Essays. Cambridge University Press, 1946. 53-99.

Argues that Boswell was driven by a desire for self-improvement and a zest for life to attempt to preserve as much experience in his journal as possible. A sympathetic and tolerant reading reveals Boswell's uncertain sense of himself--his habit of seeing himself as different persons, of instructing himself to assume their characters. His habitual use of the second person is evidence of a double consciousness: he is both actor and spectator, though it is as the detached observer of the journals that he lives most fully. Deprived of his father's approval, Boswell sought the guidance of "more congenial" mentors--Hume, Blair, Lord Kames, Rousseau, Voltaire, Paoli, and Johnson--and in the Life composed an "almost involuntary tribute of a great human weakness to a great human strength"--his need and Johnson's authority. Boswell was likewise motivated by a scientific curiosity in life and human nature to seek out and record intense experience. While he inevitably falls short of his ideal--to translate life completely into language--Boswell's inclusiveness, especially in the journals, his unself-consciously direct style, his dramatic sense--these make for a record of "unparalleled reality" and "unrivaled veracity."

541. Coleman, William H. "The Johnsonian Conversational Formula." Quarterly Review 282 (1944): 432-45.

Enumerates those attributes Johnson found essential in good conversation and, drawing on Boswell's Life and Hebrides, illustrates those qualities--broad knowledge acquired through wide reading, accurate and vigorous expression, imagination, and resolution--in Johnson's own conversation.

542. McCutcheon, Roger P. "Johnson and Boswell Today." Addresses Made Before the Friends of the Howard-Tilton Memorial Library of Tulane University. New Orleans: N.p., 1944. 16-28.

Asserts that Boswell, contrary to Macaulay's influential judgment, was--as his private papers confirm--both "a considerable literary figure" and "a very great man."

543. Osgood, Charles G. "An American Boswell." Princeton University Library Chronicle 5 (1944): 85-91.

Calls attention to the Memorial Containing Travels Through Life or Sundry Incidents in the Life of Dr. Benjamin Rush, which contains anecdotes and observations concerning a number of eminent eighteenth-century figures, including Boswell, Johnson, and Goldsmith.

544. Gray, W. Forbes. "James Boswell in the Newer Light." Quarterly Review 283 (Oct. 1945): 456-67.

Describes the literary undertakings Boswell contemplated but never completed, among them biographies of Thomas Riddiman, Lord Kames, Lord Pitfour, and Sir Alexander Dick; a Scottish dictionary; an edition of Walton's Lives; and essays on Young, Addison, and Gay.

545. Hegeman, Daniel V. "Boswell and the Abt Jerusalem: A Note on the Background of Werther." Journal of English and Germanic Philology 44 (1945): 367-69.

Describes Boswell's conversations in 1764 on the topics of theology, melancholy, and suicide with Johann Friedrich Wilhelm Jerusalem, whose son's suicide in 1772 provided Goethe with the climax of Werther.

546. Pottle, Frederick A. "The Life of Boswell." Yale Review 35 (1946): 445-60.

Examines Boswell's paradoxical reputation--the Life is considered a great work, but Boswell is not thought of as a great writer--in light of his private papers. The journals and letters reveal Boswell the author to be no mere stenographer but an imaginative, if not inventive, artist, and Boswell the man, though capable of foolish behavior and bad judgment, more complex and more intelligent than the Boswell of the Life. Calls for Boswell to be treated as the great literary artist that he is.

547. Boys, Richard C. "Sir Joshua Reynolds and the Architect Vanbrugh: A Footnote to Boswell." Papers of the Michigan Academy of Science, Arts, and Letters 33 (1947): 323-36.

Documents Reynolds's admiration for the architecture of Sir John Vanbrugh, first reported by Boswell in the Life.

548. Hegeman, Daniel V. "Boswell's Interviews with Gottsched and Gellert." Journal of English and Germanic Philology 46 (1947): 260-63.

Contrasts Boswell's impressions of Leipzig professors Johann Christoph Gottsched and Christian Furchtegott Gellert with those of eighteenth-century German students, including Goethe.

549. MacCarthy, B.G. "James Boswell: A Problem." Studies 36 (1947): 319-25.

Divides critics and biographers of Boswell into two camps: C.E. Vulliamy, representative of the anti-Boswellites, simply dismisses Boswell as insane, a schizophrenic; D.B. Wyndham Lewis and Abbott, on the other hand, both Boswellites, more sensibly acknowledge not only Boswell's personal failings but also his literary genius, his extraordinary powers of observation and sympathy, his humor.

550. Price, Cecil. "Meetings with Boswell." Times Literary Supplement, 8 Mar. 1947: 103.

Reprints an unpublished contemporary description of Boswell by Richard Fenton, a London lawyer.

551. Biancolli, Louis L., ed. Book of Great Conversations. New York: Simon and Schuster, 1948. 67-80, 106-36.

Introduces and excerpts from Boswell's journal his interview with Rousseau, and from the Life, eleven of Johnson's most memorable conversations.

552. Miller, C.A. Anecdotes of the Literary Club, "The Club" of Dr. Johnson and Boswell. New York: The Exposition Press, 1948.

Describes the formation and nature of The Club, traces its history, and introduces its members.

553. Smith, D. Nichol. "Johnsonians and Boswellians." Johnson Society Transactions 1948-49. Lichfield: 1950. 13-24.

Defines true Johnsonians as those scholars who regard Boswell's Life only as supplemental to Johnson's own writings: while Boswell's portrait does not contradict the impression of Johnson that emerges from the Rambler, Rasselas, or the Lives of the Poets, it can in no way replace Johnson's writings as a source of information about his thought and character.

554. Hunt, R.W. "The Malahide and Fettercairn Papers." Times Literary Supplement, 8 Jan. 1949: 25.

Reports that Lt. Col. Isham has done what Boswell intended--supplied the Bodleian library with a slip of paper on which Johnson corrected a couplet from "The Vanity of Human Wishes."

555. McCutcheon, Roger P. "Johnson, Boswell, and Goldsmith." Eighteenth-Century English Literature. New York: Oxford University Press, 1949. 73-93.

Surveys Boswell's published works and sketches his character, correcting Macaulay's assessment of Boswell: "the Life is great because it is about a great man, and is written by a great man."

556. Wells, Mitchell. "James Boswell and the Modern Dilemma." South Atlantic Quarterly 48 (1949): 432-41.

Traces in Boswell's journals and letters the conflict between reason and faith, skepticism and belief, intellect and emotion. Finds that when convinced of the truth of Christian doctrine, Boswell was happy; when troubled with religious doubt, he was melancholy. Although Johnson comforted him with reasonable arguments in defense of Christianity, Boswell never reconciled the conflict, never achieved peace of mind: he "went to his grave a troubled and unsettled soul."

557. Hart, Jeffrey. "Some Thoughts on Johnson as a Hero." Johnsonian Studies, Including a Bibliography of Johnsonian Studies, 1950-1960, Compiled by James L. Clifford and Donald J. Greene. Edited by Magdi Wahba. Cairo: Societe Orientale de Publicite, 1962. 23-36.

Compares Boswell and Johnson as young men arriving in London from the provinces: Boswell, giddy with the range of possibility offered by the city, delighted by the opportunity to experiment with different selves, is brought ultimately to despair by his inability to achieve any solid identity at all; Johnson, on the other hand, committed to the tradition of Augustan values by which he was shaped, heroically defends his identity against "the contradictory possibilities of his culture."

558. Horne, Colin J. "Boswell and Literary Property." Notes and Queries 195 (1950): 296-98.

Suggests that the reason for Boswell's separately off-printing Johnson's Letter to Lord Chesterfield and his Conversation with George III while the Life went through the presses was to protect these valuable sections against newspaper piracy.

559. Horne, Colin J. "Malone and Steevens." Notes and Queries 195 (1950): 56.

Calls attention to George Steevens's notice in the St. James Chronicle, apparently in response to Boswell's praise of Malone in the Advertisement of the first edition of the Life, stating that Steevens, like Malone, received no financial reward for his editing Shakespeare.

560. Smith, D. Nichol. Johnsonians and Boswellians. Lichfield: Lichfield Johnson Society, 1950.

See Item 533.

561. Mild, Warren P. "Macaulay as a Critic of Eighteenth-Century Literature." Dissertation, University of Minnesota, 1951.

Argues that Macaulay was "too blinded by prejudice to appreciate" Boswell and Johnson or to understand their literary achievements.

562. Anderson, W.E. "Young Boswell." Johnson Society Transactions 1951-52. Lichfield: 1952. 35-55.

Surveys Boswell's early life and writing, focusing on his attraction to Johnson and on the gradual development of his methods of keeping a journal.

563. Laithwaite, Percy. "A Boswellian Interlude." Johnson Society Transactions 1951-52. Lichfield: 1952. 19-34.

Suggests that Anna Seward's malice toward Johnson--so evident in the anecdotes she supplied Boswell that they were ultimately rejected--first arose in 1781 when Johnson criticized her poetic idol, John Milton, in the Lives of the Poets. Reviews the flirtatious correspondence between Boswell and Seward begun in 1784--Boswell requesting a lock of hair and information about Johnson's early years, Seward misleading Boswell as a way "to carry out her vendetta against Johnson."

564. Leigh, R.A. "Boswell and Rousseau." Modern Language Review 47 (1952): 289-318.

Considers Boswell's relationship with Rousseau as part of his lifelong quest to quell his fundamental insecurity with the approval, encouragement, and guidance of great men, of his desire to become them: plagued by spiritual doubts and fired by his reading of the Nouvelle Heloise, Boswell sought answers in 1764 from Rousseau to those questions which most troubled him--religious belief, morality and sex, "futurity." Concludes that Boswell and Rousseau shared a romantic spirit, an essential egotism, and a delight in the pleasures of memory.

565. Metzdorf, Robert F., Introduction. An Epistle, in Verses Occasioned by the Death of James Boswell, Esquire, of Auchinleck, Addressed to the Rev. Dr. J. D. by the Rev. Samuel Martin, Minister of Monimail. (Edinburgh, 1795). A reproduction of the first edition with an introductory note. Hamden, CT: Shoestring Press, 1952.

Explains that this poem by Martin, a former schoolfellow of Boswell, is valuable as a contemporary appraisal of his character and achievement: Martin notes Boswell's eccentricity, condemns his conviviality, but also recognizes his great abilities.

566. Torre, Lillian de la. The Heir of Douglas. New York: Alfred A. Knopf, 1952. 197-229, et passim.

Describes Boswell's legal and literary efforts in the Douglas Cause--the composition of comic songs, the publication of Dorando: A Spanish Tale and his own enthusiastic reviews of it, his edition of The Letters of Lady Jane Douglas.

567. Chapman, R.W. Johnsonian and Other Essays and Reviews. London: Oxford University Press, 1953.

Contains Items 167, 301, 469.

568. Esdaile, Arundell. "Boswell Redivivus." Quarterly Review 291 (1953): 94-104.

Praises Powell's revision of the Life and reviews the London Journal and Boswell in Holland, noting that they reveal Boswell to be an important figure in his own right, "the inventor of the interview," and a diarist as detailed, honest, and fascinating as Pepys.

569. Garton, Charles. "Boswell and Dr. Gordon." Durham University Journal 46 (1954): 63-64.

Provides a biographical sketch of the Reverend Dr. John Gordon, Archdeacon of Lincoln--not Chancellor, as Boswell records in the Life--who entertained Boswell in May 1778.

570. Walker, Raymond J. "James Boswell, Inquiring Reporter." Hobbies, Nov. 1954: 133, 147.

Describes Boswell's practice of interviewing illustrious men and notes an increasing interest in Boswelliana among collectors.

571. Collins, P.A.W. "Boswell's Contact with Johnson." Notes and Queries, n.s. 3 (1956): 163-66.

Estimates that Boswell spent 425 days in the company of Johnson, compared to Croker's calculation of 276 days.

572. Collins, P.A.W. James Boswell. Writers and Their Work 77. London: Longmans for the British Council and the National Book League, 1956.

Surveys briefly Boswell's life and the essentials of his character--his high spirits and melancholy, ambition, fondness for the social and intellectual pleasures of London and for the company of great men. Describes Boswell's journal as an attempt to understand his own character and praises the candor, clarity, and vividness of his observations. Surveys Boswell's published writing, paying particular attention to the ways Boswell recast material from the journal for inclusion in the Tour and the Life. Includes a select bibliography of primary and secondary sources.

573. Fifer, Charles N. "Boswell's Langton and the River Wey." Notes and Queries, n.s. 3 (1956): 347-49.

Supplements Boswell's account of Langton's finances with additional information about his business ventures.

574. Fifer, Charles N. "The Founding of Dr. Johnson's Literary Club." Notes and Queries, n.s. 3 (1956): 302-3.

Notes that Boswell attempted to date the founding of The Club but received only vague reports from Hawkins and Langton. Reynolds's engagement book indicates the actual date is 16 April 1764, not early February 1764 as Boswell states in the Life.

575. Reid, B.L. "Johnson's Life of Boswell." Kenyon Review 18 (1956): 546-75. Reprint. The Long Boy and Others. Athens: University of Georgia Press, 1969. 1-30.

Traces Boswell's friendship with Johnson and shows, despite the widespread belief that Boswell imposed himself on Johnson, who barely tolerated him, that Johnson valued Boswell most highly as a friend and companion. Suggests that Boswell met Johnson's great need for sociability and played the part of the son Johnson never had. Though disenchanted by Boswell's dissipations, Johnson never ceased to find Boswell a "superb companion" whom he always dearly loved.

576. Hunter, Richard A., and Ida Macalpine. "Alexander Boswell's Copies of The Anatomy of Melancholy, 1621 and 1624." Book Collector 6 (1957): 406-7.

Describes two copies of The Anatomy of Melancholy owned by Alexander Boswell, evidence that he may have shared his son's admiration of Burton.

577. Monk, Samuel H. "Samuel Johnson Quotes Addison." Notes and Queries (1957): 154.

Locates a source for Johnson's cynical reply to Boswell's suggestion that friends are rejoined in heaven--Addison's Cato (III, 1, 8-10).

578. Brooks, A. Russell. "The Literary and Intellectual Foundations of James Boswell." Dissertation, University of Wisconsin, 1958.

Traces the progress of Boswell's commitment to the writing of the Life and examines how Boswell's intellectual interests--religion, politics, travel, education--enriched his literary art.

579. Garton, Charles. "Boswell's Favourite Lines from Horace." Notes and Queries, n.s. 5 (1958): 306-7.

Notes that Boswell twice made use of Horace's description of how Lucilius used to keep a written record of his fortunes, first, as a motto to The Hypochondriack 66, second, on the title page of the first edition of the Life.

580. Frank, Thomas. "Two Notes on Giuseppe Baretti in England." Annali Instituto Universitario Orietales, Napoli: Sezione Germanica, 2 (1959): 239-63.

Attributes the relatively infrequent references to Baretti in the Life to Boswell's hostile and jealous attitude toward Johnson's friend and translator: when they first met at Venice in 1765, Boswell was condescending and detached; back in England, Boswell found Baretti conceited and his manners rough. The two were further estranged, first, by Baretti's complaints about Boswell's treatment of the Genoese in Corsica, and later by Boswell's belief that Baretti, acquitted of manslaughter after a fight with street ruffians, was indeed guilty and ought to be hanged.

581. Dankert, Clyde E. "Adam Smith and James Boswell." Queen's Quarterly 68 (1961): 323-32.

Traces Boswell's relationship with Smith from their meeting at Glasgow in 1759, when Boswell attended Smith's lectures on rhetoric and moral philosophy; though never intimate friends, they met occasionally, and were both members of The Club. Points out that, excluding references to Smith's relations with Johnson in the Life, Boswell wrote little of Smith besides complaints about his eulogy of Hume and some favorable references to The Wealth of Nations and The Theory of Moral Sentiment.

582. McLaren, Moray. "James Boswell." The Wisdom of the Scots. London: Michael Joseph, 1961. 244-88.

Introduces a selection of Boswell's writings in an anthology of Scottish literature by calling attention to his lucid prose style and by describing his particular kind of wisdom--naive, hopeful, humane.

583. England, Martha Winburn. "Garrick and Stratford." Bulletin of the New York Public Library 66 (1962): 73-92, 178-204, 261-72.

Provides a detailed record of the Shakespeare Jubilee in Stratford and contrasts Boswell's rapturous account with the cynical view of Charles Dibdin, one of the composers who supplied music for the festivities.

584. McElderry, B.R., Jr. "Boswell in 1790-91: Two Unpublished Comments." Notes and Queries 9 (1962): 266-68.

Prints extracts of letters from Evelyn Glanville Boscawen and Dorothea Gregory Alison to Elizabeth Montagu that seem to support Bishop Thomas Percy's claim that Boswell was shunned from "decent company" for his biographical indiscretions.

585. Pottle, Frederick A. "Notes on the Importance of Private Legal Documents for the Writing of Biography and Literary History." Proceedings of the American Philosophical Society 106 (1962): 327-34.

Demonstrates the value of private legal documents such as Boswell's unregistered deed discharging his promise, recorded in Hebrides, to grant his daughter Veronica an additional five hundred pounds as a reward for her fondness for Johnson.

586. Tillinghast, Anthony J. "The Moral and Philosophical Basis of Johnson's and Boswell's Idea of Biography." Johnsonian Studies,

Including a Bibliography of Johnsonian Studies, 1950-1960, Compiled by James L. Clifford and Donald J. Greene. Edited by Magdi Wahba. Cairo: Societe Orientale de Publicite, 1962. 115-31.

Shows affinities between eighteenth-century philosophic notions--the sympathetic imagination, the uniformity of human nature, the educational value of history, the practical benefits of self-examination--and Johnson's biographical principles, outlined in Rambler 60 and in Idler 84 and endorsed by Boswell in the Life and in his journal.

587. Pottle, Frederick A. "Boswell as Icarus." Restoration and Eighteenth-Century Literature: Essays in Honor of Alan Dugald McKillop. Chicago: University of Chicago Press for William Marsh Rice University, 1963. 389-406.

Analyzes a diploma presented Boswell by the College of Arcadia, an Italian learned academy, conferring upon him the pastoral name Icaro.

588. Werkmeister, Lucyle. "Jemmie Boswell and the London Daily Press 1785-1795." Bulletin of the New York Public Library 67 (1963): 82-114, 169-85.

Surveys Boswell's contributions to the London dailies, explains how Boswell's politics affected his treatment in the press, and summarizes the response--mostly satiric--to his Hebrides, Life, poems, and songs.

589. Golden, James L. "James Boswell on Rhetoric and Belles-Lettres." Quarterly Journal of Speech 50 (1964): 266-76.

Notes Boswell's admiration for the rhetorical masters of his age--Locke, Lord Mansfield, Pitt, Blair--and summarizes his views on the elements of a good style, effective oratory and elocution, as well as his opinions on drama, poetry, and history. Concludes that Boswell, though not an original thinker, was an informed and penetrating student of rhetoric and belles-lettres whose writings provide an invaluable account of eighteenth-century figures, practices, and beliefs.

590. Pottle, Frederick A. "Boswell Revalued." Literary Views: Critical and Historical Essays. Chicago: University of Chicago Press for William Marsh Rice University, 1964. 79-91.

Asserts that in light of the discovery of Boswell's private archives--journal, correspondence, book manuscripts--the reading public will learn what scholars have long known: Boswell was an intelligent man, a thoughtful and imaginative--if not inventive--writer, and "extraordinarily modern" stylist, combining average human perception with "great expressive power."

591. Ross, Ian. "Boswell in Search of a Father? Or a Subject?" Review of English Literature 5.1 (1964): 19-34.

Considers Boswell's troubled relationship with his stern, authoritarian father an archetypal father-son conflict. Shows that Boswell sought substitute fathers, first in Lord Kames, whose life he contemplated writing, and then in Johnson, who offered Boswell worldly wisdom, affection, and, most important, encouragement to write. Suggests that Boswell was able to satisfy his need for a father by imaginatively creating an acceptable replacement in the Johnson of the Life.

592. Brauer, George C., Jr. "Johnson and Boswell." CEA Critic 27.4 (1965): 1, 10, 12.

Describes Boswell and Johnson's common passions--London, conversation, truth, the Stuarts, subordination--and afflictions--melancholy, troubled relationships with their fathers.

593. Osborn, James M. "Edmond Malone and Dr. Johnson." Johnson, Boswell and Their Circle: Essays Presented to Lawrence Fitzroy Powell. Edited by Mary Lascelles. Oxford: Clarendon Press, 1965. 1-20.

Describes Malone's role in the composition of Hebrides and the Life: offering editorial advice, supplying Boswell with documents, encouraging him to keep at his task.

594. Rae, Thomas I. and William Beattie. "Boswell and the Advocates' Library." Johnson, Boswell and Their Circle: Essays Presented to Lawrence Fitzroy Powell in Honor of His Eighty-Fourth Birthday. Oxford: Clarendon Press, 1965. 254-67.

Traces Boswell's association with the Advocates' Library, now the National Library of Scotland, but in the eighteenth century a library for lawyers: he was acquainted with several librarians--Thomas Ruddiman, Hume, Alexander Brown; he read widely among both its legal and general collections; he socialized there; and in 1784, he was appointed one of five curators of the library.

595. Spector, Robert D. "Boswell's Original Preface, Enlisting the Aid of Dr. Johnson." Satire Newsletter (Spring, 1965): 122-23.

Renders an imaginary dialogue between Boswell and Johnson on the subject of Johnson's early biographers.

596. Brooks, A. Russell. "The Scottish Education of James Boswell." Studies in Scottish Literature 3 (1966): 151-57.

Describes the education Boswell received at James Murdell's private school, the University of Edinburgh, and the University of Glasgow--his acquaintance with Addison and Latin poetry, his introduction to logic, rhetoric, and moral philosophy. Shows that Boswell felt that his education was deficient but believes he underrated his learning: his own writing reveals his wide reading in English literature, travel writing, history, and philosophy.

597. McCollum, John I., Jr. "The Indebtedness of James Boswell to Edmond Malone." New Rambler C1 (1966): 29-41.

Describes the assistance that Malone, a trusted friend and selfless literary advisor, provided Boswell: he assisted in the preparation of Hebrides for publication and in its revision for a second edition; he advised Boswell in business, legal, and personal matters; and, most important, between 1785 and 1791, he provided so much practical editorial advice and moral support for Boswell that it is doubtful that the Life would have been published without his efforts.

598. Reed, Joseph W., Jr. "Boswell and the Major." Kenyon Review 28 (1966): 161-84.

Surveys the military and criminal careers of the confidence man Major James George Semple, Boswell's client and the subject of his last journal entry.

599. Winnett, Canon A. "Johnson and Hume." New Rambler: Journal of the Johnson Society of London C1 (1966): 2-14.

Considers Boswell in the role of intermediary between Johnson and Hume, representatives of medieval orthodoxy and modern skepticism, moving back and forth between them, repeating to one what the other said, provoking each to comment on his intellectual antagonist, seeking in vain for relief from his own doubts about religion and futurity.

600. Cole, Richard C. "The Sitwells and James Boswell: A Genealogical Study." Genealogists' Magazine 15 (1967): 402-6.

Traces the common ancestry of Boswell and the twentieth-century Sitwells.

601. Cruttwell, P. "Pottle's Boswell." Hudson Review 19 (1967): 683-88.

Praises Item 28 for its focus on Boswell as a writer, a man engaged in "preserving and recreating on another plane of reality the world, life and people" he had known. Suggests that the most useful approach to Boswell's writings is the adoption of "a useful fraud," the assumption that they are fictional, a vast picaresque novel. Thus, Boswell is the unreliable narrator whose supple style is the medium for his Richardsonian analysis of character and motive.

602. Fussell, Paul. "The Memorable Scenes of Mr. Boswell." Encounter 28.4 (1967): 70-77.

See Item 646.

603. Kerslake, John. Mr. Boswell. London: National Portrait Gallery, 1967.

Reproduces portraits of Boswell, his family, and his friends in an illustrated survey of his life in this catalogue of a 1967 exhibition at the National Portrait Gallery of Scotland, 18 August-16 September, and at the National Portrait Gallery, 13 October-30 November.

604. Ryskamp, Charles. "James Boswell." Four Oaks Library. Edited by Gabriel Austin. Somerville, NJ: Privately printed, 1967. 11-18.

Describes the Boswell collection of Donald and Mary Hyde at their Four Oaks Farm library, second only to the archive at Yale: first editions of Boswell's publications, presentation copies of the Life, manuscripts, memorabilia, and portraits.

605. Bronson, Bertrand H. "Samuel Johnson and James Boswell." Facets of the Enlightenment. Berkeley and Los Angeles: University of California Press, 1968. 210-40.

Believes that Boswell was haunted by "radical insecurity," by a "sense of his own insufficiency" and that he found in Johnson the strength and moral instruction he so desperately needed. Suggests that Johnson recognized Boswell's need for support, enjoyed his sincere veneration, and appreciated his good humor and curiosity.

606. Hartley, Lodwick. "A Late Augustan Circus: Macaulay on Johnson, Boswell, and Walpole." South Atlantic Quarterly 67 (1968): 513-26.

Shows that Macaulay's denigration of Boswell and Johnson in his review of Croker's edition of the Life echoes Horace Walpole's attacks on them in his letters. Notes that Macaulay's portraits are falsified and distorted caricatures; they are "superb rhetoric" and therefore "difficult to dispel completely."

607. Pottle, Frederick A. "The Writing of a Biography: Boswell's Earlier Years." Transactions of the Samuel Johnson Society of the Northwest 2 (1968): 4-14.

No library subscribing to the OCLC international data base--including the Library of Congress--reports to have this volume.

608. McAdam, E.L. "James Boswell." Johnson and Boswell: A Survey of Their Writings. Riverside Studies in Literature. Boston: Houghton Mifflin, 1969. 185-251.

Provides appreciative introductions to Boswell's major works--the early journals, Corsica, Hebrides, and the Life--calling attention to memorable passages and noting how innovative and even daring Boswell's dramatic method was.

609. Nussbaum, Felicity A. "The Literary Opinions of James Boswell." Dissertation, Indiana University, 1970.

Regards Boswell as a perceptive and sometimes innovative critic who shared many of Johnson's critical principles but still maintained independent opinions, more characteristic of the late eighteenth century than Johnson's: he valued emotion and imagination more than reason, emphasized the power of literature to capture immediate sensory experience rather than to teach a moral lesson, and, in his own biographical writing, focused more on particular details than on universal truths.

610. Ryskamp, Charles. "Boswell and Walter James: Goethe and Daniel Malthus." Eighteenth-Century Studies in Honor of Donald F. Hyde. Edited by W.H. Bond. New York: Grolier Club, 1970. 207-29.

Attributes A Defence of Mr. Boswell's Journal; of a Tour to the Hebrides; in a Letter to the Author of the Remarks Signed Verax, an anonymous pamphlet published in 1785 in response to an earlier attack on Boswell, to Walter James of Denford, the author of an anonymous novel called The Letters of Charlotte During Her Connexion with Werther (1786).

611. Siebenschuh, William R. "Form and Purpose in Boswell's Biographical Works." Dissertation, University of California, Berkeley, 1970.

See Item 621.

612. Brooks, A. Russell. James Boswell. Twayne's English Author Series 122. New York: Twayne, 1971.

Portrays Boswell as a "soul divided," attracted to both the worlds of London and of Scotland, and believes this Scotch-English tension shapes his literary career. Summarizes each of Boswell's literary works: poems, pamphlets, periodical essays, Corsica, Hebrides, the Life, and journals. Includes a chronology and selected bibliography.

613. Brown, Anthony E. "The Literary Reputation of James Boswell to 1785." Dissertation, Vanderbilt University, 1971.

Summarizes contemporary criticism of Boswell's works before the Life and notes that, in general, Boswell's reputation was favorable.

614. Lamont, Claire. "James Boswell and Alexander Fraser Tytler." Bibliotheck 6 (1971): 1-16.

Prints extracts from Tytler's commonplace book and correspondence detailing his ultimately successful attempt to persuade Boswell to suppress his name in an unflattering anecdote included in Hebrides. Describes Tytler's use of materials collected by Boswell in his Life of Kames (1807).

615. Riely, John C. "Bozzy and Piozzi: The History of a Literary Friendship and Rivalry." Dissertation, University of Pennsylvania, 1971.

Traces Boswell's friendship and rivalry with Piozzi from 1786 to 1791. Draws upon Boswell's private papers, the manuscript of the Life, Piozzi's marginalia and correspondence, and the writings of contemporaries to evaluate the authenticity of the two biographers. Concludes that Boswell's charges of inaccuracy are often unwarranted, inspired by jealousy and resentment.

616. Sawyer, Paul. "Johnson and Boswell: The Not So Odd Couple." CEA Critic 33.2 (1971): 12-14.

Characterizes Boswell's relationship with Johnson as symbiotic rather than parasitic: Boswell needed a father figure, a confessor, and a moral guide; Johnson found a lively young man who shared his passion for London, literature, and law, and whose sexual excesses vicariously satisfied his own needs.

617. Brady, Frank. "Boswell's Self-Presentation and His Critics." Studies in English Literature 12 (1972): 545-55.

Points out that Boswell, though acknowledged to be the world's greatest biographer, continues to be patronized by critics, Macaulay's caricature having fixed the image of Boswell the man which persists in various forms even today. Though esteemed by many of his contemporaries as a friend and recognized by some as a great writer, Boswell sometimes misjudged the responses evoked by his characteristic frankness. Believes that Boswell has been misunderstood because of his presentation of himself in his writing as naive, thus dividing readers' responses: some feel superior, while those capable of distinguishing man and writer feel "empathy, amusement, and admiration for his skills as a writer."

618. Dowling, William C. "The Boswellian Hero." Studies in Scottish Literature 10 (1972): 79-93.

See Item 638.

619. Gibbons, Mark Leigh. "Identity as Literary Device: Self-Presentation in Five Eighteenth-Century Writers." Dissertation, Rutgers University, 1972.

Claims that Swift, Hume, Boswell, Johnson, and Cowper in their semi-autobiographical writings employ fictional devices of self-presentation: they invent their own characters and conceive of their lives as stories. Boswell's journals reveal his desire to seek situations in which he could perform as a literary character and thus lose his own identity.

620. Riely, John C. "Lady Knight's Role in the Boswell-Piozzi Rivalry." Philological Quarterly 51 (1972): 961-65.

Reexamines the story, first recorded by Lady Phillipina Knight in her copy of the Life and since repeated by modern scholars, that Lady Knight, having heard Piozzi read from her Anecdotes before sending them to the printer, recommended that she delete a passage of abuse directed at Boswell. Shows that, in fact, by the time that Lady Knight heard the passage, the book was already at the printer, where the passage was deleted by Samuel Lysons without the authorization of Piozzi.

621. Siebenschuh, William R. Form and Purpose in Boswell's Biographical Works. Berkeley: University of California Press, 1972.

Argues that each of Boswell's three major biographical portraits "is a separate and formally distinct literary achievement." The portrait of Paoli serves the purpose of Corsica, a piece of propaganda meant to win support for the Corsican cause; Boswell shapes his material so as to portray Paoli as the embodiment of noble Corsican virtues, a modern Lycurgus, a man of judgment and courage, a champion of liberty and democracy. The portrait of Johnson in Hebrides reflects the basic strategy of that text: the juxtaposition of Johnson and his Scottish environment. Again and again Boswell emphasizes--often with a ludicrous effect--the contrast between a static stereotype of Johnson, moralist, Tory, Londoner, and his rude Highland surroundings. In the Life, on the other hand, Boswell creates a complex, interpretative portrait of Johnson as an intellectual and moral hero. Boswell's selective dramatizations and descriptions--even of Johnson's disagreeable traits such as his temper or his physical awkwardness--are guided by Boswell's understanding of Johnson's heroic character and contribute to a reader's vivid experience of Johnson's greatness. Concludes that Boswell's development, then, is not, as it has so often been represented, a linear progression culminating in the Life; each work reflects a unique purpose and employs particular methods. Boswell's success in these works demonstrates that his greatest ability as a biographer is not factual accuracy but rather creative interpretation.

622. Yung, K.K. "The Association Books of Johnson, Boswell, and Mrs. Piozzi in the Johnson Birthplace Museum." New Rambler: Journal of the Johnson Society of London 11 (1972): 23-44.

Describes the books associated with Boswell--six from his own library and another he presented to Anna Seward--now in the library of the Johnson Birthplace Museum in Lichfield.

623. Dowling, William C. "The Boswellian Hero." Dissertation, Harvard University, 1974.

See Item 638.

624. Cole, Richard C. "James Boswell's Agreeable Mr. Eccles." Philological Quarterly 54 (1975): 533-37.

Confirms an identification first made by Croker but rejected by Hill of Isaac Ambrose Eccles as an Irish literary man who attended Boswell's dinner at the Mitre on 6 July 1763 with Johnson, Goldsmith, Davies, and Ogilvie.

625. Ingram, Allan. "A Study of Imagery and Melancholy in the Writings of James Boswell." Dissertation, University of Nottingham, 1975.

See Item 647.

626. Riely, John C. Samuel Collings' Designs for Rowlandson's 'Picturesque Beauties of Boswell.' Printed for The Johnsonians, 1975.

Calls attention to the work of Samuel Collings, who collaborated with Thomas Rowlandson on the Picturesque Beauties of Boswell...Designed and Etched by Two Capital Artists. Reproduces for the first time four of Collings's drawings, previously attributed to Henry William Bunbury: "Frontispiece," "Walking up the High Street," "Chatting," and "Scottifying the Palate."

627. Bruss, Elizabeth W. "James Boswell: Genius and Stenography." Autobiographical Acts: The Changing Situation of a Literary Genre. Baltimore: Johns Hopkins University Press, 1976. 61-92.

Contrasts Boswell's explorations of his dynamic self in the London Journal with his rendering of Johnson's static character in the Life, showing that in autobiographical and biographical writing, Boswell's handling of time, portrayal of Johnson, narrative strategies, and style differ, reflecting his different purposes: in the Life, to preserve the essence of Johnson, in the London Journal, to record his own subjective experience as immediately as possible.

628. Daiches, David. James Boswell and His World. New York: Scribner's, 1976.

Provides an overview of Boswell's life and writing for the non-specialist, paying particular attention to Boswell's "search for his true identity." Includes ninety-nine illustrations of Boswell, his contemporaries, London, and Edinburgh.

629. Davies, R.T. "Samuel Johnson, James Boswell, and the Romantic." Literature of the Romantic Period, 1750-1850. Edited by R.T.

Davies and Bernard G. Beatty. New York: Barnes & Noble, 1976. 1-18.

Contrasts Boswell's imaginative and emotional responsiveness--his indulgence in "solitude and devout meditation" at Iona is characteristic--with Johnson's more intellectual, social, and cultivated response to nature and experience.

630. Radner, John B. "The Youthful Harlot's Curse: The Prostitute as Symbol of the City in 18th-Century English Literature." Eighteenth-Century Life 2 (1976): 59-64.

Contrasts Boswell, whose attitude toward prostitutes is ambivalent--he feels sympathy, yet engages them, assuming nothing can be done--with Goldsmith, Fielding, Wordsworth, and Blake, who portray prostitutes as symbols of "the perversity of human relationships in the city."

631. Bell, Robert H. "Boswell's Notes Toward a Supreme Fiction: From London Journal to Life of Johnson." Modern Language Quarterly 38 (1977): 132-48.

Examines the degree to which Boswell achieves aesthetic distance and control in the London Journal and finds that "the crucial distinction between participant and observer fluctuates and becomes blurred"--Boswell is not a reliable narrator. Characterizes the London Journal as a search for self but argues that Boswell never discovers a single consistent identity; rather he explores a variety of roles and poses, leaving readers skeptical as to the amount of self-awareness he actually possesses. Believes that in the Life, Boswell handles the dual roles of observer and participant more effectively: his protean character serves as a foil to Johnson's stable character; his judgment is more mature than in the London Journal; and in writing a biography, he has the advantage of working in an established genre with well-known conventions and a clear tradition.

632. Lustig, Irma S. "The Friendship of Johnson and Boswell: Some Biographical Considerations." Studies in Eighteenth Century Culture 6 (1977). 199-214.

Argues that "though the friendship of Johnson and Boswell is not equal, it is more balanced than many have assumed." Johnson enjoyed Boswell's admiration and was moved by his kindnesses; the two men shared a passion for literature and a devotion to the craft of writing; Boswell's good humor relieved Johnson's gloom, and his philosophic, political, and artistic ideas stimulated Johnson's intellect. Even Boswell's ode on the supposed nuptials of Johnson and Thrale does not necessarily prove that the friendship was not characterized by "enduring respect, sympathy, and harmony": Boswell, who could never resist burlesque, perhaps found his sense of "comic incongruity" aroused by serious speculation of marriage and was not necessarily expressing deep unconscious hostility.

633. Moore, Raymond Ledbetter, II. "Confession in the Life and Writing of James Boswell." Dissertation, University of South Carolina, 1977.

Suggests that Boswell used writing, both public and private, as a means of purging his guilt born of the conflict between an emotional attachment to morality and a physical commitment to gambling, drinking, and whoring. Unable to find comfort in religion, Boswell turned to friends as confessors: Oglethorpe, Dalrymple, Hume, Voltaire, Rousseau, Wilkes, Paoli, Temple, and Johnson.

634. Andrews, Stuart. "Boswell, Rousseau and Voltaire." History Today 28 (1978): 507-515.

Describes Boswell's interviews with Rousseau and Voltaire in 1764.

635. Batten, Charles L. Pleasurable Instruction: Form and Convention in Eighteenth-Century Travel Literature. Berkeley: University of California Press, 1978.

Places Boswell's Corsica and Hebrides in the context of eighteenth-century travel literature: Corsica, like a number of travel books of the period, combines two conventional formats, a descriptive account and a journal; has eighteenth-century precedents, such as Henry Joutel's Journal of the Last Voyage Perform'd by Monsr. de la Sale (1713).

636. Lustig, Irma S. " 'Donaus,' Donaides, and David Malloch: A Reply to Dr. Johnson." Modern Philology 76 (1978): 149-62.

Notes that Boswell never answered Johnson's inquiries concerning Malloch's verses in imitation of Donaides and explains that the poem, an account of King's College, Aberdeen, by Professor John Ker, refers to the children of the River Don, not, as Johnson guessed, the children of a classical Donaus.

637. Rewa, Michael. "Some Obversations on Boswell's Early Satiric Ambitions." Studies in Scottish Literature 13 (1978): 211-20.

Characterizes Boswell's youthful satiric efforts, especially his attempt with Dempster and Erskine to damn Mallet's Elvira first with catcalls, then with their Critical Strictures, as "attempts to establish himself as a literary personality quite apart from the subject he treats." These efforts are doomed to failure, however, because Boswell lacks the distance and self-awareness to see that in his London Journal, and in his own pamphlet, he is the true satiric target, "the champion of taste and aesthetic values who acts like a Dunce." Only after meeting Johnson does Boswell discover a subject and a mode for which he has a true genius--the celebrative.

638. Dowling, William C. The Boswellian Hero. Athens: University of Georgia Press, 1979.

Claims that a critical reading of Boswell's three major biographical narratives, like Tom Jones and Hamlet, "self-contained worlds of motive and action," must ignore the "real" Paoli and the "real" Johnson in order to attend literary elements in these texts--point of view, symbol, theme, characterization. Suggests that literature and history are each provisional versions of reality and that a given text--Boswell's Life, for example, or Shakespeare's Richard II--may be considered either history or literature, depending on the nature of the questions one chooses to ask about it. Finds underlying each of the narratives "a single conception of the heroic character": a hero in an unheroic world, spiritually isolated, fiercely attached to the values of a vanishing past. In Corsica, Boswell depicts Paoli, "the simplest incarnation of the Boswellian hero," a Plutarchian hero, a representative of a lost Golden Age. In Hebrides, Johnson, the isolated hero, visits the primitive Highlands and indulges a romantic nostalgia for a symbolic past evoked by ruined castles and cathedrals--"a lost world of faith and heroes." In the Life, Johnson is a tragic hero; his noble resistance to the "invisible forces of moral anarchy" are doomed to failure, the Prayers and Meditations revealing the hero's dark side, his private suffering, "the cost of such resistance to mind and soul."

639. Lyons, John O. The Invention of the Self: The Hinge of Consciousness in the Eighteenth Century. Carbondale: Southern Illinios University Press, 1979.

Examines Boswell as representative of the eighteenth century's development of a concept of self: the Life illustrates biography's new fascination with what is unique and original about human character and experience; the London Journal is Boswell's characteristically Romantic and ultimately unsuccessful attempt to discover his true self--"one of the best proofs of Hume's discovery that the self cannot know itself."

640. Spalding, Phinizy. "Profile of an Old Independent: Oglethorpe as Seen in the Papers of James Boswell." Yale University Library Gazette 53 (1979): 140-49.

Examines material pertaining to Oglethorpe found among Boswell's papers--notes for a planned biography, letters exchanged between 1772 and 1779--and concludes that Boswell drew forth a side of Oglethorpe preserved nowhere else: the elderly but vivacious and witty friend and advisor.

641. Williams, Mary Elizabeth. "Oglethorpe's Literary Friendships." Dissertation, University of Georgia, 1980.

Examines Oglethorpe's relationships with members of the Johnson Circle, emphasizing his intimacy with Boswell, their correspondence, including Boswell's solicitation of Oglethorpe's literary opinions, and notes of interviews for a biography of Oglethorpe proposed by Johnson.

642. Bogel, Fredric V. "Crisis and Character in Autobiography: The Later Eighteenth Century." Studies in English Literature 21.3 (1981): 499-512.

Notes that conversion, a central element of Western autobiography from Augustine's Confessions to The Autobiography of Malcolm X, is absent from the autobiographical writings of Sterne, Rousseau, Gibbon, Franklin, and Boswell. Although Boswell longs for a tranformation of the self and even contrives rituals to effect one, he knows such a decisive moment is impossible: like his contemporaries, he did not share Augustine's faith in a "hidden order of reality capable of bursting in upon, and reversing, the course of ordinary human experience." Argues that the shift in sensibility Boswell represents is revealed in his portrayal of Johnson as heroic not so much for his deeds as for his "way of being in the world," for his "substantiality of self."

643. Cole, Richard C. "James Boswell and Robert Colvill." Studies in Scottish Literature 16 (1981): 110-21.

Describes Boswell's relationship with Colvill, a Church of Scotland minister and poet who shared two of Boswell's interests, Corsica and the Douglas Cause. Colvill wrote The Cyrnean Hero, a long poem in honor of Paoli, which includes a tribute to Boswell, and The Fate of Julia, an elegy on Lady Jane Douglas, which Boswell reviewed enthusiastically in The Caledonian Mercury.

644. Kullman, Colby H. "James Boswell and Dr. Kennedy's Lisbon Diet Drink." Mississippi Folklore Register 15 (1981): 57-61.

Describes how Boswell, afflicted with gonorrhea, traveled to London in August 1769 to put himself in the care of a Dr. Kennedy, who prescribed his famous Lisbon Diet Drink--a combination of sarsaparilla, guaiacum wood, and sassafras. Within a month, Boswell was dissatisfied, concluded that Dr. Kennedy was "a babbler," and sought treatment elsewhere.

645. Kullman, Colby H. "The Visual Appeal of Boswell's Prose." Dissertation, University of Kansas, 1981.

Analyzes Boswell's technique of employing visual elements in order to create memorable portraits, caricatures, scenes, and full-scale dramas.

646. Fussell, Paul. "Boswell and His Memorable Scenes." The Boy Scout Handbook and Other Observations. New York: Oxford University Press, 1982. 147-56.

Characterizes Boswell as remarkably modern: the inventor of the genre of the meticulously documented literary biography, a master of the spare style, a tireless self-advertiser, a writer obsessed with authenticity, and a self-conscious role player. In the great scenes in his life and journal--his interviews with Rousseau and Voltaire, his seduction of Louisa, his appearance at the Shakespeare Jubilee--Boswell reveals his love for incongruity, a love based, perhaps, on a self-division that is likewise characteristically modern. Praises Item 28 for its charming and unpretentious style, but finds fault with the structure: it is too bound by chronology; "its total shape is a large blob."

647. Ingram, Allan. Boswell's Creative Gloom: A Study of Imagery and Melancholy in the Writings of James Boswell. New York: Barnes and Noble, 1982.

Argues that Boswell habitually employs certain patterns of imagery--of machines, of warfare--in an attempt "to regulate and moderate" his melancholy. Suggests, however, that when Boswell uses imagery as an instrument of self-analysis, it leads frequently to self-indulgence and self-delusion. Only in the journals--a subjective re-imagining of the facts--does Boswell successfully balance the real and the ideal, reconcile the world of the imagination and the actual world. Shows also that in the Life, Boswell employs a variety of image patterns--animal imagery, for example--in order to heighten the emotional effect of his descriptions of Johnson and to allow a reader to experience fully his greatness.

648. Kullman, Colby H. "Boswell's Literary Caricatures: A 'Wild Imagination' Responding to 'This World of Jest.' " Transactions of the Johnson Society of the Northwest 14 (1983): 49-63.

Documents Boswell's delight and ability in drawing humorous character sketches and analyzes the techniques he employs--exaggeration, distortion, startling metaphors, mock heroic allusions--in order to expose the follies and vices of his subjects.

649. Kullman, Colby H. "James Boswell's National Stereotypes: Ethnic Folk Humor in the Eighteenth Century." Mississippi Folklore Register 17.2 (1983): 81-90.

Describes Boswell's use of national stereotypes: he himself occasionally played the part of the selfish, beef-eating, honest, and prejudiced Englishman; he recorded Johnson's jests at the expense of poorly educated, uncivilized Scotsmen, and at the 1769 Shakespeare Jubilee, he dressed as a simple, brave, and independent Corsican.

650. Kullman, Colby H. "James Boswell's Voyages at Sea." Studies in the Humanities 10.1 (1983): 22-27.

Shows that Boswell, his imagination fired by travel accounts of Cook, Hawkesworth, and Banks, expressed a lifelong enthusiasm for sea voyages. Describes Boswell's voyages--from his crossing of the English Channel to Holland in 1763--and suggests that for Boswell, such voyages offered the opportunity to seek novelty and the truth about human nature and manners and to play the role of seafarer.

651. Lambert, Elizabeth Riley. "The History and Significance of the Relationship of Edmund Burke and James Boswell." Dissertation, University of Maryland, 1983.

Traces the friendship of Boswell and Burke, Boswell's model of political success and domestic fulfillment. Boswell cultivated Burke's friendship as a means to preferment, while Burke valued Boswell as a companion. Considers how Boswell's relationship with Burke--including their eventual falling out--colored his depiction of Burke in the Life.

652. Reiss, Ila Patricia. "Samuel Johnson and Young People." Dissertation, Florida State University, 1983.

Argues that Boswell was only one of several young people with whom Johnson had mutually beneficial relationships: Johnson guided and encouraged him, and Boswell stimulated him with new ideas and perpetuated his name.

653. Schwartz, Richard B. "Johnson's Day, and Boswell's." The Unknown Samuel Johnson. Edited by John J. Burke, Jr., and Donald Kay. Madison: University of Wisconsin Press, 1983. 76-90.

Compares "the minute details" of Johnson's and Boswell's daily life in London to the routines of members of various social ranks and finds that Johnson's day, as described by Boswell, is typical of a wealthy citizen; Johnson was unusual only to the degree to which he moved among groups--the rich and powerful, the middle class, the poor. Notes that Boswell's experience in London was more uniform, his routine typical of the "well-to-do, unattached young man." Characterizes the London of Johnson and Boswell as a city of contrasts, of "high civility and barbaric brutality" and suggests that more attention needs to be paid not simply to Johnson's daily routine but to his life in London in the context of the literary associations and traditions which surrounded him.

654. Woods, Samuel H., Jr. "Goldsmith and Miss Lockwood: Boswell and Oglethorpe's Matchmaking." Yale University Library Gazette 58.3-4 (1984): 150-51.

Calls attention to previously unpublished letters exchanged in 1775 between Boswell and Oglethorpe that reveal their efforts to bring Goldsmith together with a Miss Lockwood. Though unsuccessful, their scheme was a disinterested attempt to solve

Goldsmith's financial problems by uniting him with a woman of fortune.

655. Epstein, William H. "Professing the Eighteenth Century." ADE Bulletin 81 (Fall 1985): 20-25. Profession (1985): 10-15.

Explores the professional practice of eighteenth-century studies--the influence of institutional histories, textual politics, and affiliative networks--through an analysis of the "networks of discursive practices" involved in the Yale Boswell, a project which may be viewed according to an "entrepreneurial model": the papers were acquired by Lt. Col. Isham, a tireless captain of industry, and then packaged and distributed to consumers--professional scholars--by the "Boswell factory" at Yale, a corporate enterprise which competes at the same time with the Yale Johnson for control "over whose language and whose discursive practices will dominate the twentieth-century academy's image of late eighteenth-century British literature and culture."

656. Kullman, Colby H. "Boswell's Opinions Concerning Peculiarities of Dress." Transactions of the Johnson Society of the Northwest 16 (1985): 32-41.

Demonstrates Boswell's belief that an individual's clothing reveals character and influences behavior. Notes that in his literary portraits, Boswell carefully describes the fabric, style, and color of his subjects' dress, and that he enjoyed devising costumes for himself to mark special occasions: the dress of a blackguard for the King's birthnight in 1763, Corsican attire for the 1769 Shakespeare Jubilee.

656a. Ober, William. "Johnson and Boswell: 'Vile Melancholy' and 'The Hypochondriack.' " Bulletin of the New York Academy of Medicine 61 (1985): 657-78.

Studies Boswell and Johnson's melancholy from a modern medical perspective.

Religion

657. Watts, Henry. "Boswell: Was He a Catholic?" America 56 (1936): 186-87.

Asserts that Boswell became acquainted with Catholicism as a boy in Scotland, and, though his conversion in 1760 was short-lived, he retained enough interest in Catholic doctrine "to justify the feeling that he was a Catholic, albeit one of the weaker brethren."

658. Wecter, Dixon. "The Soul of James Boswell." Virginia Quarterly Review 12 (1936): 195-206.

Analyzes Boswell's religious beliefs: his Presbyterian upbringing, his conversion to Catholicism, and his professing of the Anglican faith under the influence of Johnson, while retaining a belief in purgatory, invocation of saints, and confession. Describes Boswell's spiritual life as "a pageantry of sinning and repentence, exuberance and despair," moods of piety and religious fervor alternating with fits of remorse brought on by alcoholic and sexual excesses.

659. Phelan, Paul J. "How Truly Catholic Was Boswell?" America, 12 Oct. 1940: 47-48.

Argues that Boswell's early conversion and lifelong attraction to Catholicism represent not a rational, reflective judgment but the impulse of "a very muddled young man" seeking an escape from the gloom of Calvinism, "a matter of mood and emotion, not of religion and devotion."

660. Hamm, Victor M. "Boswell's Interest in Catholicism." Thought 21 (1946): 649-66.

Traces Boswell's involvement with Roman Catholicism from his short-lived conversion at twenty until his death, noting church visits, as well as conversations and journal entries concerning Catholicism. Suggests that even though he never abandoned certain elements of the faith--invocation of the saints, purgatory--he attended Mass not out of an adherence to dogma, but because he found there an atmosphere conducive to devotion; it made him happy to feel pious. Finds that although Catholicism appealed to him rationally and emotionally, Boswell was incapable of a commitment to the faith.

661. Stewart, Mary Margaret. "The Search for Felicity: A Study of the Religious Thought of James Boswell in the Light of the Religious Developments of Eighteenth-Century England and Scotland." Dissertation, Indiana University, 1959.

Examines Boswell's religious experience in light of eighteenth-century thought: his strict religious training, conversion to Roman Catholicism, rejection of Calvinist theology, embracing of rational Christianity, struggle to overcome doubts, and hopes for eternal life.

662. Stewart, Mary Margaret. "Boswell's Denominational Dilemma." PMLA 76 (1961): 503-11.

Shows that Boswell, though bound as a loyal Scotsman to the National Church, disliked the gloomy and undignified Presbyterian worship and objected to Calvinist beliefs in an unforgiving God, predestination, the depravity of man, eternal damnation, and original sin. Boswell preferred Anglican and Roman Catholic services and believed in a benevolent God, salvation through Christ, and the importance of moral conduct. He remained sympathetic to Roman Catholic beliefs in purgatory and the intercession of saints.

663. Stewart, Mary Margaret. "Boswell and the Infidels." Studies in English Literature 4 (1964): 475-83.

Believes that Boswell's attacks against infidels reveal how deeply he valued his faith. Boswell frequently found himself unable to answer the arguments of non-believers and maintained that one should not associate with them, though he himself sought the company of Hume and Wilkes. Shows that Boswell presents Gibbon as the embodiment of the hated infidel in the Life and employs imagery--infidels as venomous insects, robbers, wanton destroyers--that reveal his deep fear of those who threaten his faith.

664. Stewart, Mary Margaret. "James Hervey's Influence on Boswell." American Notes and Queries 4 (1966): 117-20.

Suggests that the sentiments and phrasing of Boswell's letter of consolation to his mother upon the death of his infant brother, written 17 July 1754, are based on James Hervey's Meditations and Contemplations.

665. Stewart, Mary Margaret. "James Boswell and the National Church of Scotland." Huntington Library Quarterly 30 (1967): 369-87.

Reviews the structure of the National Church of Scotland in the eighteenth century and examines Boswell's views on the issue of church patronage: always sympathetic to the common people, Boswell opposed the practice, though he never committed himself to either the Evangelical or Moderate Party. Notes that Boswell appeared only reluctantly before the General Assembly, which he described as a "vulgar and rascally court," never accepted key doctrines of the Church, and disliked Presbyterian forms of worship.

666. Rogal, Samuel J. "James Boswell at Church: 1762-1776." Historical Magazine of the Protestant Episcopal Church 41 (1972): 415-27.

Compiles from the journals a list of Boswell's visits to church in the belief that Boswell's attendance at such a variety of services--Presbyterian, Anglican, Catholic, Methodist--reveals "a man in search of himself" and provides an important glimpse into the beliefs, practices, and clergy of his day.

667. Lustig, Irma S. "Boswell and the Descendants of Venerable Abraham." Studies in English Literature 14 (1974): 435-48.

Shows that Boswell's attitudes toward the Jews in England, expressed in two journal entries describing visits to London synagogues, reflect both conventional eighteenth-century curiosity, condescension, and ignorance, as well as his own respect and sympathy, based upon his rebellious nature, compassion for the oppressed, and understanding as a Scotsman of what it meant to be an alien in English society.

Politics

668. Brady, Frank. "The Political Career of James Boswell, Esq." Dissertation, Yale University, 1952.

See Item 670.

669. Clarke, Margaret. "Boswell: Scot. Nat." New Satire Dec. 1963: 28-30.

Reprints a letter from Boswell to Frederick Hervey, the Bishop of Derby, first published in The London Chronicle for 8-10 September 1785, expressing belief that the Union had been detrimental to Scotland and that Ireland would likewise suffer from a union with Great Britain.

670. Brady, Frank. Boswell's Political Career. New Haven: Yale University Press, 1965.

Argues that "Boswell's political career is the story of a man who mistook his own nature": neither a gifted political theorist nor a skillful practical politician, Boswell nevertheless aspired to a seat in Parliament, primarily as a means to enhance his reputation. Explains Boswell's sometimes contradictory political opinions--support for the monarchy, opposition to the American war, advocacy of Parliamentary reform--and describes Boswell's political activities in Ayreshire and in the service of Lord Lonsdale.

671. Brown, Terence M. "America and Americans as Seen in James Boswell's The Life of Samuel Johnson, LL.D., and in the Letters of Johnson and Boswell." New Rambler C6 (1969): 44-51.

Contrasts Johnson's violent prejudice against the American cause with Boswell's more reasonable and logical support of it.

672. Null, Linda Jane. "Boswell's Concept of Liberty in the Era of the American Revolution." Dissertation, University of Tennessee, 1977.

Accounts for Boswell's sympathy with the Corsicans and Americans by examining his views of authority: Boswell believed the ideal government promoted mutual respect between the leader and the people; if the authority figure abused his power, subjects should resist.

673. Henderson, James S. "James Boswell and His Practice at the Bar." Judicial Review 17 (1905): 105-16.

Provides a chronological survey of Boswell's career as an advocate, based on approximately fifty of his cases included in the Scottish Law Reports.

674. Simpson, T.B. "Boswell as an Advocate." Juridical Review 34 (1922): 201-25.

Provides an overview of Boswell's legal training and career: studies at Glasgow, Edinburgh, and Utrecht; early successes and fees; appearances before the Court of Session and in both houses of parliament; Johnson's guidance in various legal questions; his declining practice, and scheme to join the English Bar.

675. Pottle, Frederick A. "Three New Legal Ballads by James Boswell." Juridical Review 37 (1925): 201-11.

Prints and attributes to Boswell three satirical ballads, one unpublished and the others published anonymously: Song, in the Character of Lord Kames, The H[amilto]n Cause, and The Douglas Cause.

676. Duke, Winifred. "Boswell Among the Lawyers." Juridical Review 38 (1926): 341-70.

Though convinced that the facts of Boswell's life are "mostly unedifying and repugnant," provides a sketch--based mainly on his correspondence--of his career as an advocate, from his studies in Utrecht through his practice in Edinburgh to his attempt to shift to the English Bar.

677. Roughead, William. "The Wandering Jurist; Or, Boswell's Queer Client." In Queer Street. Edinburgh: W. Green and Son, 1932. 103-67. Reprint. Rascals Revived. London: Cassell, 1940. 129-83.

Sketches the career of James Gilkie, an eccentric and litigious attorney for whom Boswell in 1777 acted as counsel in Rule vs. Smith, Gilkie's unsuccessful attempt to prosecute three men for the murder of Alexander Rule.

678. Ramsay, James. "Boswell's First Criminal Case: John Reid--Sheep Stealer." Juridical Review 50 (1938): 315-321.

Describes Boswell's successful defense of John Reid in 1766 on the charge of stealing sheep and his unsuccessful defense of him on the same charge in 1774. Recounts Boswell's frenzied activities between Reid's sentence and hanging: his repeated attempts to obtain a confession from Reid, his drafting of "The Case of John Reid" for publication as a broadside, his commissioning of a portrait of Reid, and his scheme to resuscitate Reid after his hanging.

679. Murray, John. "Some Civil Cases of James Boswell, 1772-1774." Juridical Review 52 (1940): 222-51.

Provides details concerning each of Boswell's civil non-political cases mentioned in the journals between 1772 and 1774, concluding his practice at the Scottish Bar "was by no means unsuccessful."

680. Lowry, Walker. "James Boswell, Scots Advocate and English Barrister." Stanford Law Review 2 (1950): 471-95.

Surveys Boswell's career--a "plodding failure"--to demonstrate that the professional life of an eighteenth-century lawyer "was largely drudgery and routine, small problems and small cases, a disheartening search for clients and for fees."

681. Lyall, Alexander. "The Case of Dr. Memis v. Managers of Aberdeen Royal Infirmary. With Reference to Boswell's Life of Johnson and with New Material Concerning the Case from Boswell's Legal Diary and the Minutes of the Aberdeen Royal Infirmary." Medical History 4 (1960): 32-48.

Describes the suit of John Memis against the Aberdeen Royal Infirmary for naming him Doctor of Medicine in a charter that translated the same Latin phrase elsewhere as Physician. Boswell, Memis's counsel, sought advice from Johnson, argued the case before the Court of Sessions, and lost.

682. Bond, W.H. and Daniel E. Whitten. "Boswell's Court of Session Papers: A Preliminary Check-List." Eighteenth-Century Studies in Honor of Donald F. Hyde. Edited by W.H. Bond. New York: Grolier Club, 1970. 231-55.

Provides a bibliography of Boswell's printed legal papers.

683. Ives, Sidney. "Boswell Argues a Cause: Smith, Steel, and 'Actio Redhibitoria.' " Eighteenth-Century Studies in Honor of Donald F. Hyde. Edited by W.H. Bond. New York: Grolier Club, 1971. 257-65.

Examines Boswell's legal papers and ultimately unsuccessful arguments in behalf of the seller of a horse forced to take the animal back because it was said to be unsound.

684. Kullman, Colby H. "James Boswell, Compassionate Lawyer and Harsh Criminologist: A Divided Self." Studies on Voltaire and the Eighteenth Century 217 (1983): 199-205.

Contrasts Boswell's compassionate practices as a lawyer--"his legal aid to the downtrodden"--with his harsh theories as a criminologist--he advocated executions in the most violent and shocking manner. Describes Boswell's lifelong preoccupation with executions, the sight of which, he hoped, would fortify his mind against the fear of death but in fact drove him time and time again into despair. Suggests that the spectacle of a hanging, however horrifying, provided the vivid sensation Boswell require to free himself from "his frequent periods of gloomy inertia."

685. Cole, Richard C. "Young Boswell Defends the Highlanders." Studies in Scottish Literature 20 (1985): 1-10.

Analyzes Boswell's role and examines the documents in the cause of Macdonell vs. Macpherson, in which Boswell pleaded unsuccessfully on behalf of Alexander and Ranald Macdonell, who had been removed in 1767 from their ancestral lands. Believes that Boswell's vigorous participation in the cause reveals his Jacobite leanings, sympathy for the underdog, and commitment to the idea of family.

Author Index

Subject Index